From
EXECUTIVE
to
ENTREPRENEUR

Making
—the—
Transition

GILBERT G. ZOGHLIN

amacom
American Management Association

Library of Congress Cataloging-in-Publication Data

Zoghlin, Gilbert G.
    From executive to entrepreneur : making the transition /
Gilbert G. Zoghlin.
        p.   cm.
    Includes index.
    ISBN 0-8144-5010-5
    1. Executives.   2. Entrepreneurship.   3. Industrial management.
4. New business enterprises—Management.   I. Title.
HD38.2.Z64   1991
658.4'21—dc20   91-16038
                                                                          CIP

Printing number

10 9 8 7 6 5 4 3 2 1

To my wife,
Cari,
who kept the faith

Contents

Preface

Some years ago, a well-known *Fortune* 500 company was in the midst of downsizing and early-retiring thousands of employees, many of whom were mid- and upper-level managers. It was a difficult process for the corporation, and it had brought in an outplacement firm to help the departing personnel. The outplacement firm, in turn, asked my firm—Engler, Zoghlin, Mann, Ltd.—to provide exiting employees with financial-planning information and services.

As employee-benefits/financial-planning consultants, we'd done a bit of this sort of work before, but not on such a large scale. After talking with many of the downsized executives, I was astonished. I had assumed that virtually all of them would be eager to find another corporate job. Some of them were, but many others told me they weren't sure whether they wanted to return to the corporate world. In fact, a significant percentage were interested in starting their own business.

In the following years, I worked with thousands of other downsized employees from a variety of corporations throughout the country. In each instance, the same issues were raised—managers who had worked for companies for ten, twenty, and even thirty years were seriously considering becoming entrepreneurs. The more I thought about this trend, the more it made sense to me. The number of corporate jobs—especially middle-management jobs—was shrinking fast. Small businesses were booming. These ex-executives possessed skills and experience that would serve them well as entrepreneurs. They also had significant financial resources from severance packages and employee-benefit programs.

During one-on-one financial-planning sessions with departing executives, a single question kept coming up: "Do you know where I can find some information about making the transition from being a corporate executive to running my own business?" I had no answer. The standard literature on entrepreneurship didn't necessarily apply to former executives. Their situations were different. They approached the entrepreneurial world with their own set of advantages and disadvantages, opportunities and traps. In short, they were in a different category from other entrepreneurs. It struck me that a book addressed to individuals facing this decision was sorely needed.

In the course of writing this book, I've interviewed many former corporate managers who have tried to become entrepreneurs. Some have succeeded, some have failed, and the jury is still out on others. The people I've talked to represent a cross section of corporate jobs and entrepreneurships. They include everyone from CEOs to junior executives; their businesses range from restaurants to consultancies. What unites them is their corporate past. It is a significant determinant—perhaps the most significant determinant—of how they'll do on their own.

Throughout this book, I'll use words such as *corporate* and *ex-executive*. Although these terms are convenient, they can also be confusing. In this context, *ex-executive* simply refers to anyone who has worked for someone else. You may have been a top manager for a huge corporation or a lower-level employee of a small, family-run business. The common denominator is that you used to work for someone else. What I have to say, then, applies to *all* former employees, regardless of job title or size of company.

In this book, I'm not going to give you a blueprint for setting up your own business. There are plenty of books and other materials that can help you do that. Nor am I going to discuss such admittedly important nuts-and-bolts issues as how to write a business plan or set up an accounts-receivable system or create effective advertising. Instead, I'm going to focus on the transition from executive to entrepreneur. How do you escape the mind-set of an employee and adopt the mind-set of an employer? How can you best translate the skills you acquired as a corporate employee to an entrepreneurial setting? How can you determine whether you're really suited to running your own business? What mistakes do ex-executives commonly make when they become entrepreneurs, and how can you avoid them? These and other questions define the cutting-edge issues, and I will address them in a way that will help you make a well-informed decision about your career.

The book is divided into four parts:

1. "Making the Decision" gives you a sense of the trade-off that's involved—employee for entrepreneur—and the implications of that trade-off. By the end of the part, you should have a better idea of whether you're ready to become an entrepreneur.
2. "How Your Past Will Affect Your Future" contains four chapters. The first helps you select an entrepreneurial path. The following three chapters concentrate on the psychological and practical consequences of that choice: handling entrepreneurial decision making, acquiring a special kind of discipline, and avoiding traps that executive-entrepreneurs often stumble into.
3. "Cases in Point" examines the four common categories of executive-entrepreneurships: consulting, retailing, product sales, and special situations (from franchises to hobby-based businesses).
4. "Transitional Tools" focuses on such nitty-gritty issues as securing funding and creating tax strategies. As a former executive, your approach to these issues will differ significantly from that of a nonexecutive. I've limited my discussion to the considerations that are most relevant to executive-entrepreneurs.

Finally, it might surprise you to learn that I'm not advocating that corporate employees desert their employers in droves to start their own ventures. On the contrary, I've tried to keep this book free of proentrepreneurial bias because my research has clearly demonstrated that many people are suited to work for others, but only some are suited to work for themselves.

I hope to help you determine what suits *you* best. When people make the right executive-versus-entrepreneur decision, both established corporations and new, entrepreneurial companies stand to benefit. Large corporations are more productive if they're staffed by people who really enjoy being corporate employees. Similarly, entrepreneurial entities are more productive if they're run by people who love being entrepreneurs rather than by ex-executives who secretly wish they could rejoin the corporate world.

These pages reflect a basic optimism. I believe that large companies are on the right track as they streamline their operations, consolidate positions, and operate leaner and cleaner. There are numerous opportunities for talented, ambitious corporate managers. There are numerous opportunities for entrepreneurs as well. As you'll see in Chapter 1, the golden age of entrepreneurs is about to dawn, and it's an age in which ex-executives will play a critical role.

ONE

Making the Decision

These first three chapters are crucial, no matter whether you've made the decision to become an entrepreneur or are merely considering it.

If you have already made the decision, the material in Part One gives you a chance to double-check that decision—to consider the current entrepreneurial environment and trends and whether you're ready to capitalize on them. If you are merely considering the idea, this part should help you determine whether an employee or an employer mind-set suits you best. After reading these three chapters, you'll be in a position to analyze your choice objectively.

Chapter 1 gives you a sense of the forces fueling the shift from executive to entrepreneur. In it, I explain why so many corporate managers are leaving their organizations and setting up shop on their own.

Chapter 2 is filled with self-testing devices, which permit you to determine whether your experience, expertise, and emotional makeup put you in a good position to make the transition from executive to entrepreneur.

Chapter 3 ends the part on a cautionary note, waving a yellow flag before all of you who are ready to rush forward. In it, I list the arguments against becoming an entrepreneur, detailing the difficulties other corporate executives have had in trying to make the switch. Such a chapter might seem odd given this book's theme, but it's necessary, believe me. I've seen too many people leave great jobs at great companies to start their own business, only to realize many months and dollars later that they were better off where they were. If you happen to fall into this group, I hope Chapter 3 saves you some time, money, and misery. If Chapter 3 convinces you that you're *not* in this group, then you can proceed with confidence.

Chapter 1

The Golden Age of Entrepreneurs

Historically, entrepreneurs have been a breed apart from the stereotypical businessperson. They were gutsy, innovative, iconoclastic risk takers who prized their independence. Some of the best-known entrepreneurs—the Mellons, Goulds, Carnegies, and Fords—could be ruthless. They didn't hesitate to bend or break the rules to get what they wanted.

Corporate executives, in contrast, played the business game by the numbers. The reason they joined corporations in the first place was to avoid risks, to go after realistic rewards, to achieve attainable goals, to be part of a team. It was comfortable working for a large organization. They had access to plentiful resources. They received approbation from higher-ups and the satisfaction of climbing a corporate ladder, together with perks and periodic raises.

Best of all, they were given jobs for life. Contrary to myth, the "full-employment" concept didn't originate with the Japanese. It's as American as apple pie. When people joined the corporation, they received a de facto contract stating that as long as you don't screw up, it's unlikely you'll be asked to leave. The corollary to that contract was: Give the organization trust, loyalty, and effort, and you'll be rewarded with security.

People rarely left that security. Who would want to give up a job for life, with the resources, prestige, and responsibilities of working for a corporation? Who would want to leave all that for an uncertain future? Not many, especially in light of statistics claiming that most start-up companies fail after one year.

But things change. The most basic change in corporate America is that the de facto contract between employer and employee is defunct. In an era of mergers and acquisitions, leveraged buyouts, downsizing, and foreign competition, no one has a job for life.

Although that came as a shock to many corporate employees, it shouldn't have. The job-for-life concept wasn't a treasured tradition, passed down from one corporate generation to the next. In fact, not so many years ago, the rugged individualism of entrepreneurs was the rule in business rather than the exception. Household servants and serfs were loyal, not corporate executives. It has only been in the last fifty years that unswerving corporate loyalty became an accepted fact of organizational life.

Things change, though, and they change quickly.

It wasn't so long ago that the United States made the most popular automobiles in the world, the German camera and the Swiss watch outsold all others, secretaries preferred typewriters to computers, and corporate executives had jobs for life.

The economic, social, and technological changes that have occurred over the last twenty years have affected every corporation. The giants of industry have fallen, or at least been weakened. U.S. Steel (now part of USX Corporation), for instance, began struggling against foreign competition. Its obsolete mills employed far more people than Japanese and Swedish mills. To fight that competition, USX designed new mills that required fewer workers and were less costly to run.

As is always the case, the first workers to lose their jobs were those closest to the product—those who made the steel, worked on the assembly line, packed, and shipped. For a while, white-collar executives were safe. But not for long. The pressure was on to streamline, to cut staff positions. At first, voluntary measures such as early retirement were employed. Then, when more cuts were needed, pink slips began appearing on the desks of executives who had thought they were impervious to layoffs.

No one expected it. But because the corporation naturally felt responsible for breaking the defacto contract with its executives, the trauma was cushioned by generous severance packages. In addition, the corporation had beefed up its benefits programs—savings plans, retirement plans, stock options, and stock bonuses. Consequently, when executives departed the corporation, they weren't empty-handed. In many cases, they left with six- or even seven-figure sums.

Picture yourself as one of these suddenly jobless executives with a good deal of money. You may be in the prime of your corporate life, years away from retirement. You've received the best training the organization had to offer. You've acquired a network of contacts as well as superior management skills.

One more thing: You've become a risk taker. When you were downsized out of the company—or when you saw your office mates being axed—your illusions about job security were shattered forever. You realized that although holding a middle-management position with a *Fortune* 500 company might reduce risk, it doesn't eliminate it. Even if you find a great job with another company, even if you have a powerful mentor and a vice-president's title, you're still vulnerable. All it takes is a hostile takeover, a downturn in the economy, a new, cost-conscious CEO, and you're out of a job.

You make a logical assumption: Whatever I do, I'm going to be taking a risk, so why shouldn't I take that risk *outside* of the corporation? The risk might be greater, but so, too, are the rewards. I have money, skills, and contacts. Why don't I invest them in myself, in my own business? A new breed of entrepreneur is born.

This isn't a hypothetical scenario. Every year, thousands of executives facing similar situations are becoming entrepreneurs. They represent a break from traditional entrepreneurs. They're not seat-of-the-pants wheeler-dealers, lacking formal business training and in debt up to their necks. They have far more advantages than previous generations of entrepreneurs. Their capital, connections, and business savvy make their entrepreneurial dreams achievable. Instead of launching a business on a wing and a prayer, they have access to lines of credit; computerized models; and inventory, manufacturing, and finance skills. Compared to entrepreneurs of the past, the odds of their success are high.

The golden age of entrepreneurs is dawning. Some of the most experienced businesspeople are forsaking corporations or being forsaken by them. As a result, the talent pool from which entrepreneurs are drawn has never been deeper. Entrepreneurial businesses are growing by leaps and bounds, representing a major shift in business power and resources. More executives are leaving their organizations to become entrepreneurs than ever before.

There is every indication that this entrepreneurial movement will not only continue but grow. Foreign competition isn't going away; merger and acquisition activity will probably increase; marketplace pressures will make corporations want to run even leaner and meaner. The days when corporate executives had jobs for life are gone forever.

Furthermore, entrepreneurial opportunities are expanding at an astonishing rate. No longer does society regard the entrepreneur as an outsider. Entrepreneurs are the new American heroes. Books are written by and about them. Magazines detail their exploits. Venture-capital firms exist to fund their efforts. Associations and other support groups are springing up to help them. Even corporate America has acknowledged the entrepreneurs' contributions, expressing admiration for their risk taking and attempting to incorporate the entrepreneurial spirit into corporate culture.

If you're a corporate executive, you're probably aware of your precarious position and the entrepreneurial possibilities. If you haven't yet decided to make the switch, you've probably thought about it. You'll probably think about it even more in the weeks and months ahead. Should you do it? If so, how do you make the transition from corporate team player to entrepreneur? What entrepreneurial paths are available to an ex-executive? How do you capitalize on your corporate contacts and skills to increase the odds that your venture will be successful? This book is designed to help you answer those and other critical questions.

First, you must understand that you can't follow other entrepreneurial models. You can't attempt to duplicate the steps taken by someone with only a high-school education who managed to turn a $5,000 loan into a multimillion-dollar business. You can't suddenly shed your corporate skin and become a high-stakes gambler. The legacy of your corporate past has influenced you in both positive and negative ways.

You must understand the effects of that legacy and take those effects into account in embarking upon an entrepreneurial venture. Psychologically, you have a big adjustment to make when you leave the corporate womb. There are also significant financial, management, and social adjustments. You have to prepare yourself to overcome your corporate mind-set and start thinking and acting like a rugged individualist. It's not easy, and it's not for everyone. Part One helps you determine whether it's for you.

Another crucial issue is what type of entrepreneur you want to be. Some of you will want to start a business totally divorced from the corporation—an antiques store, a hot-dog stand, or a bed-and-breakfast hotel. Others will become consultants, keeping close ties to the industry you left. Still others will become involved in equity deals with smaller companies or franchise operations. Whatever type of business you choose, even if it's far removed from your former job, your corporate-acquired skills will prove invaluable. How to use those skills and leverage your contacts is discussed in Part Three, "Cases in Point."

As an entrepreneur, you become a very different type of manager than in the past. Gone are the memos and meetings, the paper objectives and vast resources. Most of you will be managing yourself and a handful of employees, at least at first. You're going to have to reorient your thinking when it comes to running the business. For example:

> ‣ How will you deal with hiring and firing without a personnel staff to assist you?
> ‣ How will you handle your first real crisis without a crisis-management team in place?
> ‣ How will you respond to situations requiring you to make decisions in hours or days rather than weeks or months?

Considering these questions in advance should help you avoid the mistakes of many neophyte entrepreneurs.

Throughout the book, I'll use examples that illustrate typical situations. You'll read about ex-executives who failed and succeeded in their entrepreneurial endeavors—e.g., a former *Fortune* 500 exec who opened a microbrewery, a human resources director who purchased a temporary-employment franchise. Although each of the ex-executives is different, you'll see something of yourself in all of them. How these men and women capitalized on or were defeated by their corporate past is instructive.

I'll also sketch the entrepreneurial paths available for ex-executives—paths that you can choose based on your interests, abilities, and attitudes. They're not well-worn paths, however. Five or ten years ago, very few executives would have so much as considered stepping outside their office towers to venture down them. Even today, although the numbers are growing, only a small percentage of corporate managers have trod these paths. But things change. The exodus from the corporation has begun. We're going to see more and more people like you exploring entrepreneurial territory.

If you have spent years behind the protective walls of a large organization, the journey can be terrifying and exciting, difficult and rewarding. You need a guide for such a journey, and I believe this book will serve you well. By the time you finish reading it, you'll be in an excellent position to decide whether you should make the transition from executive to entrepreneur.

Chapter 2

Are You Entrepreneur Material?

As you sit in your office, imagine being the sole survivor of a shipwreck, stranded on a deserted island. One moment you were on a luxury cruise ship, sipping piña coladas, beckoning the ship steward to fetch you another pillow for your deck chair. All your needs were provided for: abundant, delicious food; entertainment; exercise. There was always something going on: dancing, friendly faces, social activities.

Suddenly, all that disappears. You find yourself lying on a sandy stretch of beach. When the shock wears off, you begin dealing with questions of survival you never had to consider before: food, shelter, a hostile environment.

But survival isn't the only issue. Can you adapt to the isolation? Can you maintain your morale, your motivation? Finally, if no rescue is in sight, it becomes a question of whether you can thrive in this new environment. Can you find ways to take advantage of the island's natural resources? Can you enjoy your new life? Could you spend the rest of your days here and be as satisfied with your new life as you were with your former life? Do you think you might be able to be even *more* satisfied than you ever were before?

I think you get my point. The journey from executive to entrepreneur is a perilous one. Some of you are well-equipped to make that journey; others are not. The subject of this chapter, however, is whether you *should* make it.

Key Questions

Not everyone should strike out on their own. Maybe an entrepreneurial work style sounds great—no bosses, no bureaucracy, freedom from rigid structures—but the reality can be a shock. Therefore, before bidding the corporation adieu, you should ask yourself a series of questions designed to assess your chances of making it as an entrepreneur.

How Do You Feel About the Corporation?

How much are you going to miss the corporation after you leave it? If you've been fired or downsized—or if you're fed up with the politics and red tape—then your initial response might be: Not at all! But that initial response could be misleading.

Consider the case of Mark Cryden, a vice-president with a major packaged-goods company. Twice during the last five years, he had been passed over for promotions. The first time, the president told Mark he wasn't "senior enough." The second time, the president explained that he didn't have the temperament to handle the position.

For twelve years, Mark had been a solid corporate citizen. He enjoyed his job, the people he worked with, the work environment. Yet when Mark was passed over for a promotion the second time, he was angry. Although only forty-four years old, Mark knew others his age who had jobs with more responsibility, more prestigious titles, and higher salaries.

Mark had a friend who worked for a venture-capital group. For a few years, that friend had been encouraging Mark to break away from the corporation. Every few months, the friend would mention a new business the venture group was backing and ask Mark whether he were interested in running it.

After the second missed promotion, Mark was ready. Like a jilted lover, he was eager to begin a new relationship. Mark left the corporation to manage a start-up company marketing gourmet frozen-food products. Even though he only had five people working for him and a first-year operating budget of under $1 million, Mark did well. After six months, Mark was actually able to forecast a slight profit for year's end, with excellent prospects for expansion and increased profits in the second year.

There was only one problem: Mark missed the daily routine of corporate life—the meetings, the lunches with colleagues, the battles for a bigger slice of the budget, even the political infighting. He missed participating in the high-powered decisions and being part of a company that was in the public eye. It wasn't that he hated entrepreneurial life. It was just that he didn't like it enough. After a year, Mark resigned and was hired as a vice-president at another *Fortune* 500 company.

MORAL: THERE'S NO PLACE LIKE HOME, AND HOME IS WHEREVER YOU'RE MOST COMFORTABLE.

In one sense, it's easier to give up the perks, salary, and staff than it is to jettison the intangibles. The move from executive to entrepreneur isn't like changing companies; it's like changing life-styles. Some executives thrive on the action surrounding a multimillion-dollar new-product introduction; they relish the corporate gossip; they look forward to presenting a program to ten top executives. If you have an empty feeling in the pit of your stomach at the thought of losing those things, don't become an entrepreneur. Far better if you:

- Can't stand the corporate culture
- Can't stand to see one more meaningless memo
- Stare at the clock as a meeting drones on endlessly
- Distance yourself from corporate politics and avoid playing the requisite games

If this sounds like you, chances are good that you'll enjoy the entrepreneurial life-style.

Are You a Solid Corporate Citizen?

It's not only how you view yourself within the corporate context. It's how the corporation views you.

Within any organization, there are people who don't seem to "fit." Some are cynics, frequently mocking the higher-ups. They're the ones who scoff at the rules and regulations, who poke fun at the brownnosers and the company's hallowed traditions. Others don't display their negative attitudes so overtly. Some are looked on as "independents," who don't work particularly well in groups and function far better if left to their own devices. Some are simply outspoken, willing to buck trends and the prevailing opinion. A case in point is the executive who rises in a staff meeting and says, "I know everyone is excited about the CEO's new plan, but I just don't see how it's going to work."

And there are those who, at one time, might have been solid corporate citizens but have now lost the faith. Downsizing, mergers, early-retirement programs—all the trends in corporate America discussed earlier—have changed their attitudes. What once attracted them to corporate life—security, loyalty both received and given, high morale—has disappeared. They don't feel at home in the streamlined organization. They're anxious to work in a different environment.

Why Are You Leaving the Corporation?

Are you leaving because you really have your heart set on being an entrepreneur? Or is it because you can't stand your boss? Or because you're dissatisfied with your position or your salary? Or because the notoriously incompetent director who had the office next to yours left and is making a million a year with a used-car business and you figure if that idiot can succeed, it should be a piece of cake for you? Or because you just feel confined or have an irresistible urge to be on your own?

I've found that the executives most likely to succeed as entrepreneurs are the ones who leave because they've got a great idea for a business. They can't stand sitting in their office one more day letting that idea stagnate. The idea is an obsession, something they can't get out of their mind, something they think about during every spare moment. Like any entrepreneur, you'll need a tremendous amount of energy, and that idea can be thought of as an energy source, an inexhaustible supply of fuel that will compensate for all the resources you'll lack as an independent businessperson.

Ironically, it helps if you come up with a great idea and are then conveniently downsized out of a job. Downsizing has numerous effects, but one of the most beneficial from an entrepreneurial standpoint involves money. If you're a mid-level executive or above and have been with a company for a significant period of time, you're likely to get a hefty benefits payment when you're downsized. If you're fortunate, you'll also be given access to financial planners as part of the outplacement process. Those two advantages could give you a running start on your entrepreneurial career.

Are You a People Person?

If it seems silly to ask whether you're a people person, consider that the majority of successful entrepreneurs are extroverts who love talking to anyone and everyone—from janitors to judges. Whether or not they know it, this is a critical skill. To keep their business moving and growing, they have to establish numerous relationships, because unlike a corporate executive, they can't rely on relationships that have been in place for years. They're constantly talking to customers, suppliers, bankers, lawyers, accountants, partners, technicians. They have to be able to communicate well with a wide variety of people in all environments.

Many executives lack this ability. It's not that they're bad communicators; it's simply that they only feel comfortable communicating with certain people in certain ways. Honestly ask yourself whether you feel ill at ease when talking to somebody outside your department. If you're a manufacturing executive, do you have difficulty dealing with ad-agency types? Are you intimidated by CEOs or other top-ranking people? Do you find yourself at a loss for words when you're in an elevator with people you don't know?

I know of one executive who always assumed she was a master communicator. A sales manager, she gave great motivational speeches to her sales force. She fired off sharp, easily understandable memos. She was a virtuoso with the telephone, milking the instrument for all it was worth. But when she left the company and opened up her own small business, she ran into a roadblock: She couldn't communicate (and didn't like communicating) with equals.

This sales executive was terrific when dealing with subordinates or higher-ups within the company; she had the lan-

guage down cold. But when it came to dealing with outsiders—
with sources of referral business, for instance—she was a fish
out of water. She didn't know what buttons to push to get a
response; she felt uncomfortable because other people weren't
attuned to her way of thinking. When she was trying to set up
a deal with a potential customer, the vendor told her point-
blank: "Sally, I don't think we can work together. Our styles of
doing business are just too different."

To a certain extent, what business you choose determines
the type and variety of people you deal with. If you open a
store, for instance, you'd better be prepared for a never-ending
stream of customers, suppliers, maintenance workers, and
many others. But even if you open a consulting business, you're
still going to have to hustle, to "network." Some of you are
natural networkers. Others can acquire the skill. But some of
you will find it an impossible or enervating task. If that's the
case, think twice before taking the entrepreneurial plunge.

Can You Handle a Different Type of Stress?

In corporations, most of the stress an executive feels is generated by external forces: a boss, a deadline, a written set of
objectives, a competitor's move. Entrepreneurial stress, on the
other hand, is more internal than external. It's often self-
imposed. If you've been used to constantly achieving goals
within the corporation, how will you react when your fledgling
company doesn't grow as fast as you anticipated? When you
find you have to tell your financial backer that you overesti-
mated your first-year profits and need more money? When you
can't meet your payroll or a customer files a lawsuit against
your company?

As a corporate executive, you can isolate business problems from your personal life (at least, many executives can).
Let's say you're an MIS executive who's been lobbying for the
purchase of a new computer system. You know that the system
will greatly improve inventory control, yet management vetoes
the purchase, saying the system costs too much. Sure, you're
mad. Certainly, you grouse about the decision. But life goes on.
As an entrepreneur, though, you'll take these things much

more personally. If you find you can't afford a new computer system, you'll be more than angry; you'll be frustrated because you know the purchase would be a terrific boost for your business. And your ego will be wounded. Is there something wrong with you that you can't generate enough income to buy the system? Maybe you don't have what it takes!

Practically every entrepreneur is going to have a series of setbacks. Rarely do things proceed according to plan. Far more than a corporate executive, an entrepreneur's self-worth is linked to his or her job. When you lose a customer, that customer is rejecting *you*, not the corporation!

How will you handle this stress? Is your self-image strong enough to withstand the inevitable assaults upon it? If you've got that inner strength, then you'll have a critical entrepreneurial advantage.

Is This the Right Time to Make Your Move?

When you leave the corporation to become an entrepreneur, external pressures should be minimal. If you're trying to put three children through college or face big loan payments, those financial pressures will intensify when you're on your own. If you're going through a divorce, undergoing psychotherapy , or trying to kick a drinking problem, it may well be the wrong time to start a business.

Determine whether now is the time to become an entrepreneur. Think about what's happening—or will soon be happening—in your life. As difficult as this seems, it could be advisable to postpone your corporate leave-taking for a few months or even a few years.

Fred Willoughby is one fellow who chose not to postpone the decision, even though he and his wife had just had twins. A strategic planner for one of the country's largest import-export companies, he decided to leave in order to open an antiques store that would import French country-style furniture. Money wasn't a concern; Fred had arranged a sizable bank loan and had received benefits and compensation in the mid-six-figure range when he left the company. And his store did well right from the start, becoming a trendy place to shop.

The only problem was that Fred had underestimated the travel requirements. He had anticipated spending no more than four or five days a month traveling. Unfortunately, it turned out that he was away from home two weeks out of every month. Not only did Fred feel guilty about not being able to watch his babies grow, but his relationship with his wife was terribly strained. She resented his long absences and bitterly complained about them more than once. Ultimately, Fred sold the business and rejoined the corporate world.

The moral of this story isn't that you should wait until you're free of all obligations before becoming an entrepreneur. It's simply that you should assess the realities of the situation before making a move.

Do You Really Want to Be Your Own Boss?

"I *love* being my own boss!" is an entrepreneurial refrain. This is especially true of small-business owners who used to be executives. They'll talk your ear off about their freedom from corporate committees, political power plays, and insensitive bosses. Their perorations about being one's own boss have an almost messianic quality.

Do you share those sentiments? Before answering that question, consider that the concept of not having a boss is a bit misleading. An entrepreneur does have a boss, albeit not in the traditional sense. As an entrepreneur, you will literally be working for yourself. What do you think of yourself as a boss? You may well feel compelled to work yourself harder than the toughest CEO in any corporation. You may demand more of yourself than you can possibly deliver, unrealistically expecting perfection. You might be content with your performance as an executive but find that you don't measure up when you're on your own.

Or listen to a vice-president of an industrial-products group who started an independent distribution organization: "I used to report to this guy who was a miserable demanding SOB. Now, I have ten customers who are just like him." Clients, customers, partners, and investors can turn into bosses. They are as capable of making your life unbearable as any small-minded, self-serving executive who stalks a corporation's corridors.

What type of boss you like to deal with can be a good indicator of your potential for success as an entrepreneur. Some of you enjoy playing the subordinate-boss corporate game. When it comes to bosses, you don't take their remarks and actions personally. If they're jerks, you know how to forge political alliances so they can't hurt you. If they're mediocre, you turn the tables on them, putting them in the position of being dependent on you. If you're this sort of person, you might be best-suited for corporate life.

On the other hand, you might not have the patience or ability to play this game. You'd rather deal with bosses who don't have absolute control over your career, who can't unilaterally negate your decisions. In most instances, entrepreneurs can cut ties to customers and others they can't stand. Or they can suffer the fools gladly, since their contract with them is limited. In either case, the entrepreneurs, not their boss, control the relationship.

The Final Question

Do you look forward to being an entrepreneur the same way you look forward to that first real job after graduation? If you don't, if you have second thoughts about leaving the corporation, then you might want to reconsider your decision. You're going to need all the enthusiasm of a fresh-faced kid to drive yourself to success. When things get tough, you don't want to second-guess yourself and think, "I should have stayed where I was." If you do, you'll probably cut your entrepreneurial career short prematurely and return to your executive niche. You won't give yourself enough time to succeed.

Go back and think about the questions posed in this section of the chapter. Try to answer them honestly. You might even ask them of friends or coworkers to get their perspective on whether you're entrepreneur material.

Key Questions

- How do you feel about the corporation?
- Are you a solid corporate citizen?
- Why are you leaving the corporation?
- Are you a people person?
- Can you handle a different type of stress?
- Is this the right time to make your move?
- Do you really want to be your own boss?
- Do you look forward to being an entrepreneur the way you looked forward to your first real job after graduation?

You don't have to score 100. You might have doubts about a few of the answers and be unsure about whether you fall on the executive or entrepreneur side of the line. That's okay. The purpose of these questions is to give you a sense of your entrepreneurial qualities. If you have some of these qualities and not others, you may nevertheless do very well on your own. If you can't develop some of these qualities over time, you may be able to get along without them or hire people to fill in the gaps.

Ultimately, the questions posed here will allow you to make an informed choice between an executive and an entrepreneurial career. After answering them, your instincts should take over and give you a feeling about where you belong. If you find that an executive position suits you best, stop reading, put this book on the shelf, and wait a few months or a year. Then ask yourself the questions again; the results may be different next time. I have a hunch, however, that most of you will fall on the entrepreneurial side of the line. If so, sit back, keep reading, and get ready to learn how to enter a brave, new world.

Your Corporate Breakaway Potential (CBP)

Are you really going to feel comfortable with a job outside of a corporation? Although it's hard to answer that question until you actually step into the entrepreneurial world, this test will help.

The following questions are designed to give you a CBP reading. Answer them honestly and instinctively. After you've done so, use the suggested answers for each question and the CPB index to grade yourself and determine the likelihood of your becoming a successful entrepreneur.

Questions

1. *How many consecutive years have you worked in a corporate environment?*
2. *When you first decided to become a corporate executive, what was your motivation?*
3. *If your boss told you that you were being terminated next week, how would you react?*
4. *If you could change one thing about your job, what would it be?*
5. *What are some of the corporate policies and practices you don't agree with?*
6. *How do you feel you're perceived by other corporate employees?*
7. *When you meet people at a party and they ask you what you do, how do you feel about what you tell them?*
8. *If you left the corporation and your entrepreneurial business failed, would returning to a corporate job be an option you'd consider?*
9. *Every corporation has a culture. What words would you use to describe yours?*
10. *How would you describe your relationship with your boss?*
11. *If you left the corporation, what would you miss most?*
12. *If your CEO granted your fondest corporate wish—the job, salary, and perks you've always dreamed about—how would that dream job compare to the option of starting your own business?*

Answers

1. *If you've worked between five and twenty years at your corporate job, give yourself a point. That's usually enough time*

to accumulate a significant amount of assets to use in your entrepreneurial enterprise. It's also enough time to have gained sufficient skills for use in your new business. I've found that those who leave with less than five years' experience tend not to have the necessary skills and monies and those with more than twenty years' experience have too much invested in the company to leave.

2. *Give yourself a point if you answered "security." I've found that many ex-executive entrepreneurs were originally attracted to corporate life because of the security—job, financial, etc.—it promised. Because that security no longer exists, many executives no longer have their original motivation to remain with the corporation.*

3. *If your reaction would be a mixture of relief and anxiety, add another point. You don't get a point if you would only feel anxiety.*

4. *I've found that the single thing most successful executives who made the corporate break would change is their relative lack of power. Most were extraordinarily frustrated by their inability to impact the company's direction. You can also give yourself a point if you answered "more decision-making authority, more clout, less bureaucratic red tape."*

5. *Appropriate answers include "decisions by committee; memo writing; frequent meetings; rigid rules regarding hours, expense accounts, etc.; unfair bonus structures." If you named one or more of these, give yourself a point.*

6. *One point if others perceive you as any or all of the following: an outsider, a troublemaker, not a team player, an iconoclast, a contrarian.*

7. *You feel a certain embarrassment about what to do. You find yourself steering conversation away from your job and company. You don't take any great pride when others recognize your company's name or are impressed by your job title. You don't receive a point if you boast about the company or your position in it.*

8. *No. The correct answer is that you'd try to find another business to start up. Executives who become entrepreneurs don't regard it as a one-shot deal; they make a commitment to an entrepreneurial path.*

9. *Your corporate culture is inbred, encourages cutthroat competition, values teamwork over individual stars, favors conformity, encourages a patriotic loyalty to the company, insists upon a step-by-step progression up the company ladder. Again, one or more of these earns you a point.*
10. *Many high-potential entrepreneurs have a rocky relationship with bosses. The problem is that the budding entrepreneurs believe they can do their bosses' job better than the bosses, that they're not allowed to shine because of the restrictions their bosses place on them.*
11. *"The money, the perks, the glamour"—all are acceptable answers. If you answered "the interactions with other employees, the chance to work with large budgets, the satisfaction of achieving specific objectives and being rewarded for those achievements," you don't receive a point.*
12. *You'd respond: "It would be a tough decision, but nothing could equal the chance to be on my own." Almost without exception, entrepreneurs value their independence above and beyond anything else.*

The CPB Index

0–3 points: This low score doesn't mean you'll never be a successful entrepreneur. It does indicate, however, that you are well-suited to life as a corporate executive, that your attitudes dovetail with your role as an employee. You might want to wait six months or so and test your CBP again; the passage of time could change your score. Then again, I've known people who have scored low on their CBP and gone on to a successful entrepreneurial career. Typically, these people are "hybrids," equally comfortable working for others and working for themselves. If you sense that you're this type of person, don't worry about your score—you'll do fine on your own.

4–8 points: This middle-range score suggests that you have the potential to be a successful and satisfied entrepreneur. If you scored near the higher end of this range, you're probably ready to leave; although you might have some reservations, they pale before your very real desire to strike out on your own. If you scored near the lower end of this range, you're on the cusp. Your mixed feelings might be a cause for concern. That's not necessarily fatal to any entrepreneur, but if you find your answers demonstrate that you really relish certain aspects of corporate life, be cautious. Compare the answers for which you received a point with the ones for which you didn't. How strongly do you feel about the "points" versus the "nonpoints"? If the nonpoints involve issues that strike you as relatively insignificant, then you're probably ready to make a chance.

9–12 points: All signals say "Go!" You've got nothing to lose and everything to gain by starting your own business. You've shed your employee mind-set somewhere along the way, and you're clearly dissatisfied working for someone else. The only warning flag I'd wave has to do with overconfidence. Simply having the proper entrepreneurial attitude doesn't guarantee success. You'll face a number of decisions once you start your own business, and you can't assume you'll automatically make the right ones. As much as you might want to, you can't ignore your corporate past. It will be both a help and a hindrance. (Part Two, "How Your Past Will Affect Your Future," should enable you to make it more of the former and less of the latter.)

Note: Very few corporate executives get a perfect score—even the ones who subsequently launch a successful entrepreneurial career. So don't worry if you only scored 6. As long as you scored more than 3, you have potential. That's all you need to continue exploring entrepreneurial possibilities.

Chapter 3

No Paid Vacations

Most of you probably have a proentrepreneurial bias. You picked up this book because you're dissatisfied to some extent with corporate life, and entrepreneurial possibilities seem eminently attractive. But my purpose isn't to convince every corporate executive to become an entrepreneur. Entrepreneurship isn't for everyone. Although I've tried to give you some ways to determine whether entrepreneurship is right for you, most of this book in fact offers advice and tools that will help you successfully make the transition from executive to entrepreneur, and the underlying assumption is that you want to be an entrepreneur. In this chapter, however, I describe the other side of the coin—specifically, why certain people should remain executives and not strike out on their own.

During my discussions with executive-entrepreneurs, outplacement counselors, and others, I've heard the horror stories about executives who wasted frightening amounts of time and money in doomed quests to become entrepreneurs. Therefore, before you commit resources to your own business, consider the cautionary lessons of this chapter. Despite downsizing, a shrinking middle-management class, and steadily eroding job security, corporations offer many advantages that entrepreneurships cannot. It's possible that your attitudes, abilities, and circumstances dictate a corporate career. Don't forsake the corporation until you've carefully examined the downside of being an entrepreneur.

What You Give Up

Too often, in deciding to leave the corporation, executives concentrate on what they will gain, not what they will lose.

You're going to lose more than you might think. Here are some of the losses that certain executives find unacceptable:

▸ *A Regular Paycheck.* Years ago, a friend of mine worked for a company in a staff position and decided to transfer to sales. As a salesperson, he still had an office in the company's headquarters but received a sales commission rather than a paycheck. After a few weeks in sales, he transferred back to his old job. The problem: He couldn't stand to see everyone receive a paycheck on Friday when he received nothing.

The biggest problem is psychological—reorienting your thinking so you're not dependent on a regular paycheck. it's scary to watch your bank balance dip without a predictable bimonthly infusion of cash. Although you may receive a check for twice what you made as an executive, it may arrive weeks or even months after you expected it. The waiting period can be agonizing, especially if you've spent years living from one paycheck to the next.

▸ *Resources.* As an entrepreneur, you probably won't have a large staff, extensive computer capabilities, a range of expertise to draw upon. In most instances, if you want something done, you'll have to do it yourself. You can obtain all the resources available at the corporation, but as with the perks (discussed below), they come at a premium price. Some people are accustomed to having resources at their fingertips and run into trouble when they must either make an effort to search out resources or even to do the job personally instead.

▸ *Personal Time.* As a general rule, entrepreneurs work longer hours than executives, especially when they're first starting a business. And they often work different hours than corporate executives. Your nine-to-five schedule might suddenly become seven to seven; you could find yourself regularly working on weekends. For executives accustomed to the time structure of the corporate workplace, the entrepreneur's longer, unstructured work routine can be a shock.

▸ *Paid Vacations.* Entrepreneurs don't take vacations; they take time off and pay for it later. When you go on a two-week vacation, you'll find yourself working extra hard when you get back to make up those two weeks—the hours you put in at night and on weekends will equal your vacation time. Some ex-executives don't mind. Others longingly remember when vacations didn't have consequences.

‣ *Action.* One of the things that attracts executives to big organizations is the opportunity to occupy center stage. Your company's moves are covered by the trade press; you participate in deals involving millions or even billions of dollars; you're introducing products on the cutting edge of technology.

There's also the social action. You become part of a large community with its own culture. You're involved in company politics; in the gossip of your workplace; in the lives of scores of subordinates, higher-ups, and peers. Your spouse and family may also be involved.

Until entrepreneurs build large organizations of their own, they're cut off from much of this action. It's like moving from a large city to a farm in the middle of nowhere. The odds are that as an entrepreneur, you'll never duplicate the action of a big company.

‣ *Perks.* The company car, the frequent-flyer airline mileage, the big office—these are just a few of the corporate perks that don't automatically come with an entrepreneurial job. *Automatically* is the key word. Obviously, as a successful entrepreneur, you can provide yourself with all these perks and more. But you have to pay for them. Initially, you probably won't be able to afford all the perks you received at your former company. Even when you *can* afford them, you may find that the money could better be spent elsewhere.

‣ *Status.* You're no longer senior vice-president of operations for a well-known *Fortune* 500 corporation. I've known many executives who relished their titles and their association with a well-known entity. To a certain extent, it defined who they were. As a titleless consultant, for instance, you forsake that definition.

How Do You Feel About All This?

The previous seven points are emotional issues, not practical ones. You don't need extensive resources, perks, or action to do

well as an entrepreneur. If you have sufficient income from
your new business, you can acquire much of what you've lost.
The key question is: How do you feel about these seven losses?

Don't try to determine if you can handle it, if you can
adjust. You probably can, but that's not the point. The point is:
Do you want to? Are you going to resent the losses? Are you
going to miss what you no longer have?

An entrepreneurial business, far more than a large organization, rises or falls on the basis of the owner's attitude toward
the business. Remember, you'r going to be under a great deal
of stress. That stress, combined with your longing for the
advantages of a corporate job, can rob you of your energy and
initiative. You need that energy and initiative. As the owner of
your own business, you have to make things happen. You don't
have the luxury of sitting back and waiting for success to come
to you. You've got to be on the phone and on the road, constantly looking for ways to bring revenue into your company.
If you're depressed, disappointed, lethargic, or indifferent, it's
not going to happen.

Priorities

As you try to choose between a corporate and an entrepreneurial career track, one technique that should help you decide is
to prioritize your goals. Consider Figure 3-1, a chart comparing
the priorities of two executive-entrepreneurs. In each case, the
priorities are listed in order of importance to the executive-
entrepreneurs.

Both A and B sound like budding entrepreneurs. But B,
because of her priorities, is much more emotionally ready to
quit the corporation and stike out on her own. The reason: B's
goals can only be satisfied by becoming an entrepreneur. A's
goals, although they could be satisfied via his own business,
are more likely to be achieved within the corporation. A transfer or a job change might do the trick.

Set your goals, prioritize them, and determine whether a
corporate or an entrepreneurial career is most likely to satisfy
them. If it's a toss-up, you would probably be wise to remain

Figure 3-1. Comparison between the priorities of two executive-entrepreneurs.

Executive-Entrepreneur A	Executive-Entrepreneur B
Double my salary in the next two years.	Be my own boss.
Find a job I really enjoy.	Be involved in every aspect of the business.
Free myself from bureaucratic red tape.	Implement new ideas and be solely responsible—as well as or punished—for the ideas' success or failure.
Gain greater autonomy in my decision making.	Realize long-term financial gain.

in the corporate mainstream. An uncertain attitude toward entrepreneurship won't cut it; you need to be driven toward entrepreneurship, not drift into it.

If You're at the Top

When highly successful, top corporate executives come to me and say they want to start their own small business, I immediately question their judgment. Their entrepreneurial desire doesn't make sense on several levels:

1. They've beaten the odds and climbed the ladder to its highest rung. They're receiving a large salary; have great perks; supervise scores, hundreds, or even thousands of people; have huge resources at their command. If they wanted to, they could probably land a similar position at any one of a number of corporations. They are among the corporate elite.

2. Their position of power entitles them to a degree of autonomy and responsibility similar, in some respects,

to that of an entrepreneur. They're the ones calling the shots. To some extent, they've acquired a degree of immunity from petty corporate politics and bureaucratic red tape. Qualitatively, their standard of corporate living is high.

3. Psychologically, financially, and socially, a CEO who leaves a prestigious position to start over from scratch as a sole proprietor is toppling from the heights. Not many people can absorb the shock from such a long, hard fall.

Please don't misunderstand my words of caution. There *are* some top executives who make great entrepreneurs, who can leave their organization without regret and translate their considerable skills and contacts into a small business. It isn't easy, though. The best candidates are those who have succeeded inspite of themselves, who had always chafed under their corporate harness and yearned to be on their own. It can happen. But it can also happen that senior executives consider their entrepreneurial options only when their company is taken over or they have a falling out with their boss. Although it's possible they *shouldn't* stay at their corporation, they might be better off simply seeking a job at another corporation rather than starting their own venture.

If You're at the Bottom

Some people bloom early. There are under-thirty junior executives who leave their organizations and become hugely successful entrepreneurs, seemingly overnight. But a basic premise of this book is that the new age of entrepreneurs is going to be led by ex-executives who have accumulated substantial expertise, experience, and financial resources while working for corporations.

How much can you have accumulated if you've worked at a corporation for only a few years? Of course, if you possess a single-minded drive to become an entrepreneur, a great idea, and the seed money to implement it, experience is irrelevant. Youthful enthusiasm and energy can overcome many mistakes.

My general advice to young executives is this: Don't leave the corporation until you really understand what you're leaving. Don't let one unpleasant corporate culture or one manipulative boss drive you out. Give the corporation a chance. Once you really grasp what a corporate career is all about, you're entitled (and far better qualified) to make your decision.

Your Capacity for Entrepreneurial-Type Risk

Working for a corporation is a risky business. No corporate job is secure in this age of downsizing. But at a large organization, your risk isn't omnipresent; it hovers in the background—a possibility but not a probability. You don't have to think about it constantly, and besides, there's not much you can do about it.

Entrepreneurial risk is constant. You risk something every working day. Every decision you make, every deal you do, every person you hire—each one carries a risk. True, no one can downsize you out of a job. But you can lose money or even put yourself out of business if you blunder. What is your attitude toward and capacity for this type of risk? Some people tolerate occasional worries about the slight risk of being fired better than they tolerate the daily stress of entrepreneurial risk. How do you know whether you're one of those people?

The first part of the answer's easy. Just think about how you felt when the company announced staff cuts of 15 percent, or when rumors circulated that your corporation was about to be acquired, or when you had a bad quarter and it sounded as if the size of your department was going to be reduced. Did you agonize over the possibility of being fired? Did you hate the fact that you were about to be a victim of fate? Did you spend sleepless nights worrying about when the pink slip would arrive? Or did you refuse to let it bother you? Did you feel that even if you were terminated, you'd simply find another corporate job?

The second part of the answer's a bit more difficult. You need to project yourself into an entrepreneurial setting. Does your stomach start churning when you think about how you're going to repay your bank loan for the business? How will you react when your best customer decides to take the account elsewhere? Would you be furious if you trained someone for a year—developed someone as your chief assistant—only to see that individual leave for another job just when he or she was about to become productive?

Which type of risk do you prefer—corporate or entrepreneurial? The best entrepreneurs thrive on the latter type of risk. They're energized by its challenge. They love the fact that they have some influence over their risk. Unlike corporate executives, they exert a degree of control over the outcome.

Executives Outnumber Entrepreneurs

It's a simple fact: More people are employed as executives than as entrepreneurs. Just because the golden age of entrepreneurs is about to dawn, you shouldn't feel that you have to be there as the sun starts to rise. Statistically, the odds are in favor of your remaining an executive.

There's nothing wrong with that. Maybe you're not ready to make the move. Maybe you'll never be ready. Corporations are becoming more entrepreneurial, and you might find that your organization will provide you with opportunities to be more innovative and independent. It's possible that you're destined to be the CEO of General Motors rather than the owner of a body shop.

Don't make your decision just yet, though. Remember that this downbeat chapter is designed to provide some balance, not discourage you altogether. Remember, too, that the remainder of the book offers additional insight about executive versus entrepreneurial jobs, so keep an open mind until you've finished reading.

TWO

How Your Past Will Affect Your Future

The decisions you make as an independent businessperson will be affected, consciously or subconsciously, by your corporate past. Part Two is designed to help you avoid mistakes to which that past makes you prone as well as capitalize on what you've learned.

Chapter 4 shows you how to evaluate your business alternatives and choose the one that fits your particular needs. As you'll see, your entrepreneurial choice won't be made in a vacuum; you'll be influenced by your years as an employee when making that choice. You'll want to be sure that your decision reflects your true desires and abilities—that it's not based on a negative reaction to being downsized, for instance. And on the positive side, you'll want to select a business that enables you to take advantage of the resources you've acquired as an executive.

The next three chapters should get you over the "hump"—the crucial first year on your own that is the "make or break" period for so many ventures. Chapter 5 helps you deal with the numerous decisions you'll be called on to make—decisions that require an entrepreneurial rather than an executive mind-set. Chapter 6 helps you acquire the discipline every entrepreneur needs in order to keep your resources focused on what's crucial, rather than tangential, to your business. Chapter 7 makes you aware of the traps virtually every executive-entrepreneur faces and explains the entrepreneurial selling process (which differs considerably from the selling process within a corporation).

Chapter 4

Entrepreneurial Options: The Entrepreneurial Menu

Let's say you determine that you've got what it takes to succeed as an entrepreneur. What next? You can't just "be" an entrepreneur. There's no such thing as an entrepreneur store or an entrepreneur service. The word *entrepreneur* describes an attitude, not an actual job. You can begin by making a fundamental choice between two basic entrepreneurial paths: the path of least resistance and the path of highways and byways.

The path of least resistance, as the name implies, involves a business related to your work with the corporation. You're an MIS executive and decide to become a computer consultant; you're an advertising manager and want to open an ad agency. One way or another, you're staying in the same field but changing settings and structures. The path of highways and byways, on the other hand, involves a business unrelated to your corporate job. You're an operations manager and decide to open a hot-dog stand; you're a sales rep and want to run a bookstore. Your new venture isn't limited by what you did before; you can pick and choose from a wide variety of fields.

Which path is right for you? Figure 4-1, which compares the traits of individuals who tend to be successful in following each of these paths, may help you decide.

Your Secret Wish

There's no value judgment attached to either entrepreneurial path; one isn't inherently better than the other. It comes down to a question of what's right for you, which isn't always easy

Figure 4-1. Choosing between the path of least resistance and the path of highways and byways.

Follow the Path of Least Resistance If:

- You feel uncomfortable doing things you haven't been trained for.
- You don't hate your corporate job; you hate the corporate environment. You take great pride in the skills you've acquired as an executive. You don't like doing "new" things.
- You would like to have an agreement with your former employer to continue working for the corporation in an "outside" capacity.

Follow the Path of Highways and Byways If:

- You feel "out of place" in your corporate job; you've never felt comfortable with what you've been doing.
- You dislike the repetition, get bored solving the same problems.
- You feel confined in your job and powerless to effect changes you feel are necessary.
- You want to make a fresh start.
- The corporation consistently refuses to implement your best ideas.

---

to determine. It's all bound up in the fantasy job you've been daydreaming about at the office.

I've found that the impetus for many executives to become entrepreneurs is a secret wish, a dream they've harbored for months or years. It's the if-I-could-do-anything-I-wanted vision they keep returning to while grinding away in their office. Those wishes are great. They're highly personal and valuable, and no entrepreneur should be without one. Not only can they take you out of the corporation, but their energy can sustain you through the tough, early days of entrepreneurship.

The problem with wishes is, they don't always come true.

Your fantasy of an entrepreneurial life might not jibe with its reality. Let's say you dream about running a bed-and-breakfast in Vermont. From the confines of your city-bound office, it sounds terrific. You can imagine yourself and your family living in idyllic splendor, the kids romping in the woods, you fishing a sparkling crystal stream, your spouse filling the Victorian mansion with the smells of fresh-baked bread. The reality, however, might be decidedly different. Your kids might miss their friends; your spouse might hate the country; you might be so busy running the place that you'd never have time to go fishing.

Therefore, test your wishes before they become reality. Although it might seem more "adventuresome" and entrepreneurial to jump right in with both feet—just pull up stakes, move to Vermont, and buy the bed-and-breakfast—it might also be unwise. How can you test your wishes? There are a number of ways, the easiest being an apprenticeship. If you want to own a bed-and-breakfast, volunteer to work in one for a month or so. Whatever your dream is, you can get a taste of it. You can even do it before quitting your corporate job. Spend two weeks of vacation working in a restaurant if that's what your entrepreneurial fantasy revolves around. Talk to people who have done what you plan to do. Ask them the following questions to separate your fantasy about the business from the reality.

Fantasy-Reality Questions

1. When you started the business, what was the biggest obstacle you had to overcome?
2. If you had it to do over again, is this the business you'd choose to enter? Why or why not?
3. What pressures do you feel because of the business? How do these pressures affect you, and how do you deal with them?
4. What sort of person do you think is best-suited for this line of work?
5. If you were to open this business today, what do you think your chances of success would be?

6. What does it take to make your business successful?
7. Looking back, what could you have done to make the business easier to run?

Once you've finished your research, a useful way to evaluate the findings is to take a piece of paper and divide it into two columns; then put your feelings and thoughts about your entrepreneurial endeavor (the fantasy) on the left and the facts you've gleaned about what the business is actually like (the reality) on the right. Is there a big discrepancy between the two columns? For instance, your dream is to open a bar, and you come up with a fantasy-reality list that looks something like this:

Fantasy	*Reality*
Chance to meet interesting people	Hassles with liquor-licensing board and police
Fun	Long, late-night hours
Stimulating work environment	Untrustworthy employees
Way to make a sizable amount of money without being confined to an office	Complaints from neighbors about noise

Are you willing to tolerate the reality? Is enough of the fantasy left intact? Draw upon your corporate experience to make these determinations. Reflect on what you like and dislike about your job as an executive; these preferences are directly translatable to an entrepreneurial business. If you hate paperwork, and the reality of your new venture is that there will be tons of forms and detailed record keeping, you might want to think twice. On the other hand, if you love making deals for the corporation, and your entrepreneurial calling will demand constant wheeling and dealing, you might be making a good choice.

The point of these exercises is to make you a realist. The worst thing you can do is leave your job with unrealistic expectations—start your own business and be terribly disappointed by it. If that happens, you'll probably conclude that you weren't cut out to be an entrepreneur. But that probably isn't true! You might be a great entrepreneur if you first took a longer and harder view of entrepreneurial possibilities.

Structural Options

As an entrepreneur, you have two basic choices about how you'll set up your business: by yourself or with a partner. Of course, there are numerous variations on these two themes. Partnerships, for instance, can involve everything from equity deals to "silent"-partner money. But the big choice is between going it alone or bringing in others. Each route has significant financial, personal, and business ramifications, and you should take some time to analyze them. In Chapter 14, the issue of structure is considered from the standpoint of liability and taxation, but for the moment, let's consider this issue strictly from the standpoint of your personal work style. Here's what these two options boil down to:

- If you go it alone, you'll be in control. You'll have all the responsibility and accountability you've ever wanted. You won't have to worry about being second-guessed or hamstrung by a partner who isn't pulling his or her weight.
- With a partner (or partners), you'll gain a sounding board—someone to bounce ideas off of. A partner also brings additional expertise and capital (which you might lack). Furthermore, you won't be as tied to the business as you would if you were independent; it will be easier to take vacations, to leave the office without having to worry that the business might be falling apart in your absence.

You have to decide which structure dovetails with your personality. Again, review your corporate career. As a manager, do you like being part of a team? Do you enjoy shared responsibility? Do you ever get anxious when you have to make decisions by yourself?

Some people leave corporations precisely because they can't stand the emphasis on group objectives and decision making by committee. Others leave for totally different reasons; they don't mind sharing decision making but despise other things about the corporate environment. If you honestly evaluate your reaction to the issues discussed in this section of the chapter, you can predict which structure will best meet your needs.

Timing

Although there's no "right" time to leave the corporation, there *are* some guidelines.

First and foremost, it isn't a great idea to leave when you're under serious emotional or financial pressure. The transition from executive to entrepreneur is tough enough without carrying the added weight of a pending divorce or two kids about to enter college. Try to time you departure so that you're under as little pressure as possible.

Second, consider market and economic conditions. If you plan on becoming a semiconductor manufacturer, find out how the semiconductor market is doing. Similarly, assess the economic climate, not only nationally but in your area.

Third, give some thought to how much experience and energy you have at a given time. If you're twenty-three years old, you might be bursting with energy, but have you really had time to acquire all the skills necessary to run your own business? If you're near retirement age, you might have acquired tremendous skills but be burned out from all those years in the corporate world. The executives who make the most successful entrepreneurial transition usually have a good mix of experience and energy. They've put in their time with the organization but haven't overstayed their welcome; they still have the drive to achieve.

Fourth, and most important, the best time to leave the corporation is when you feel an irresistible urge to become an

entrepreneur. If that seems obvious, consider that many executives leave to become entrepreneurs for reasons other than a
true entrepreneurial calling: They hate their new boss; they
were passed over for a promotion; their cousin told them about
a great franchising opportunity.

Depart from your organization when you've had enough—
when a small inner voice says you want nothing more to do
with corporate life and are ready to try something on your
own. Objectively analyze your impulse for leaving. One of the
easiest ways to conduct such an analysis is to determine
whether your departure is catalyzed by a specific event (or
events) or whether it reflects a more general, deep-rooted
feeling. If it's the former, be careful. Don't make a major
change in your career based on an isolated occurrence. Your
anger at your boss will pass. When it does, what's left? You
need that gut-level certainty that you'd be better off without
the organization.

Type of Business

You can look at your entrepreneurial options from countless
perspectives, especially when it comes to the type of business
you want to start. As the saying goes, the world is your oyster.
So how do you find that pearl of a business? One good way to
begin is to examine the four major categories of entrepreneurial businesses and decide which one meets your needs:

1. Consulting
2. Retailing
3. Product sales
4. Untraditional business (far removed from mainstream
   corporate business)

Actually, there are more than just these four categories, but
I've limited the discussion to the types of entrepreneurial
businesses chosen by a majority of executives. The following
overview should serve to whet your appetite and start you
thinking about your options; then, in Part Two of this book,

"Cases in Point," these four options are examined in considerably greater depth.

Consulting

If you're starting a consulting business, will you be able to convince your former employer to be a client? If you can, it's a great idea. Neophyte consultants need both résumé and revenue. If your former employer is a *Fortune* 500 corporation, listing it as a client will impress other potential clients. Also, work farmed out to you by a former employer could provide you with an income stream as you get your business started.

Consulting also has relatively low start-up costs; you can even work out of your home at first. If you decide you don't like consulting, it's easy to walk away from it; you're not burdened with capital investment. Consulting also gives you a flexible work schedule. Aside from client meetings, you can do the work when you see fit. If you're someone who wants to spend more time with your children or have the mornings free for gardening, you can build your schedule around these activities.

For many ex-executives, one of the biggest drawbacks of consulting is the selling. Most middle managers aren't accustomed to selling intangibles—themselves and their services. They have trouble dealing with rejection, with the highly personal entrepreneurial selling process in which they put themselves on the line. Corporate executives generally are buyers, not sellers. The consulting business involves a role reversal, and it's one that some executives find demeaning.

Another problem is clients—they exist in different "neighborhoods." The corporate neighborhood consists of people who all share certain beliefs, methods of communication, goals. Each potential client represents a different neighborhood with a different and largely unfamiliar set of attitudes and beliefs. As a consultant, the executive must become a traveler, journeying into these new neighborhoods and trying to learn their customs. Some corporate executives love this sort of travel. They enjoy the selling process, the chance to learn about new people, the diversity of each day. Others find such travel alien to their nature and never really become comfortable with it.

Retailing

Most corporate types find control to be the major advantage of opening a store. Few businesses are more a reflection of their owners. You control the way the store looks, the way the merchandise is displayed, the environment, the products sold. There is a direct correlation between you and your store's success. For executives who desire this control—and who hate the lack of it at their organization—retailing is probably a wise choice.

Owning a store also gives you greater control over the competition. It's a different form of competition from jockeying with another executive for a promotion or even helping the company steal market share from another organization. In those situations, you possessed relatively little control; you were at the mercy of your boss, your company's policies, huge economic and social forces. As a store owner, though, you can compete on a more direct level. Your decisions about pricing, merchandise display, the look of the store, and its location all have an immediate impact. Obviously, you can't control everything (such as people's tastes or a changing neighborhood), but more than with virtually any other type of business, your actions can make you a winner in the competition for customers.

The biggest negative about a retailing business is the hours. Regardless of whether you're running a restaurant, boutique, or hardware store, you'll be married to the business. As more than one former-executive-turned-retailer observed, "The business eats you alive."

Another consideration is that many executives, weaned on target marketing, have to adjust to selling to everyone. As a retailer, you can't choose your customers. This means you must welcome everyone who walks through your door as a prospective buyer. Some of the people will be irritating, obnoxious, and boring. It doesn't matter; you have to treat all of them with respect and deference. Consultants have more control over who their customers are, especially after they get their business going; they can afford to be selective. Be aware that if you decide to open a store, you won't have that luxury.

One other point of comparison between retailing and consulting: Retailing is usually more lucrative. Consultants sell their time, and there are only so many hours in a day. Retailers, with good markup and volume, don't tie their profits to time.

Product Sales

If you were a product or brand manager or in sales and enjoyed the various aspects of marketing a product, you may be attracted to product sales. This entrepreneurial category contains many subsets, from being a manufacturer's rep to licensing a product to direct marketing. If you have sizable financial resources, you can handle the whole ball of wax—from manufacturing to distribution to selling (however, I've found that few executive-entrepreneurs have these resources, at least at first).

Unlike consulting, product sales provides you with something tangible to sell. Unlike retailing, you usually don't have all the headaches associated with running a store. It's a relatively clean and simple business: If you can find a good product and establish a solid customer base, you have a reasonable chance of success.

Finding a good product is a knack some people naturally have. At the corporation, they were able to pick winners with uncanny accuracy. They sensed when a product was "right" and when a specific market would be receptive to that product. If you have this knack, product sales may be a good choice for you.

On the negative side, product sales as an entrepreneur is far different from product sales as a corporate executive. As an entrepreneur, you have a far shorter time frame in which to make your product a success, you lack the clout to obtain distribution easily, and you're forced to compete against companies with much greater resources than you possess.

Another problem is falling blindly in love with your product: You mistakenly assume that because you're offering a better mousetrap, the world will beat a path to your door. But since you're a small-business owner, the world may not even be able to *find* your door. Creating awareness of the product's benefits and convincing even a small market to buy it is a long, hard process. You must have good selling and communication skills to make a splash. This is true whether you're a rep selling a line of clothing to retail buyers or a licensed distributor selling a product to a consumer market via direct mail.

Perhaps the single most important quality for someone who chooses product sales is an understanding and enjoyment of the product-selling process. It's not for everyone. Some people prefer selling a service or having the customer come to them (in a store); they're unable to muster enthusiasm for an inanimate object, be it a widget or a computer. Others, however, relish selling objects—objects that they believe in, objects that translate into a specific dollar figure per sale, objects that they can instinctively match to a certain type of prospect. If that sounds like you, start looking for your product.

Untraditional Business

The untraditional-business category is for all of you who want to make a clean break not only from your old job but from corporate life in general. You want to start a fishing-guide service in the Florida Keys; you have a burning desire to launch a bush-pilot operation in the Yukon; you dream about opening a bookstore, an exotic-car dealership, an import-export business dealing in French country antiques. Although some of these businesses might overlap with the preceding three categories, what sets them apart is that they're on a smaller scale and totally divorced from the work you did at the corporation.

The best thing about an untraditional business is starting fresh. Most of what bugged you about big business—the politics, the corporate culture, the bureaucracy, the conformity—will vanish. More than likely, you'll be fulfilling a lifelong dream and won't be doing it for money, but for love. It's a great, energizing feeling.

The flip side is that you're going to have a steep learning

curve. If you're not someone who likes to learn, watch out! Let's say you've worked for twenty years as a human resources manager and decide you want to open a jazz record store. You know the music. But do you know how to set up an inventory-control system to make sure the records, tapes, and compact disks you ordered are delivered? Have you put an antitheft system in place to guard against shrinkage? Do you have a cash-flow system?

Some things you'll have to learn on the job; other things you'd better familiarize yourself with in advance. If you open a restaurant, don't postpone finding out how to keep the place sanitary until a customer comes down with a case of food poisoning.

The fantasy-reality discrepancy I discussed earlier usually has its greatest impact in this entrepreneurial category. Prepare yourself for the shock. Do as much homework as possible before making your move so you won't be overwhelmed. Ask yourself, Do I love challenges and new projects? If the answer is yes, an untraditional business is the right choice for you.

Final Questions

Choosing an entrepreneurial alternative can be a complex matter. To make an effective choice, take a long, hard look at what you know about yourself and what you learned at the corporation. Don't ignore your years as an executive, no matter how much animosity you might bear toward that time. Examine who you are and your feelings about various issues by asking yourself the following questions, which have proved helpful to other executive-entrepreneurs:

▸ Am I burned out? If so, what accounts for the burnout? The corporate environment? Specific job responsibilities? Will my chosen entrepreneurial career avoid these same burnout factors?
▸ Is my goal to make a lot of money? If so, is it realistic for me to expect to fulfill that goal with the new business I've chosen?

- ▸ What have I enjoyed most about my corporate job? The paycheck and perks? The boss's compliments for a job well done? Implementing or supervising? Dealing with people or creating strategies by myself in the office? Will my new business provide similar enjoyment?
- ▸ What has made me most uncomfortable? What aspect of my corporate job did I dread? Will my new career allow me to avoid similarly uncomfortable situations?
- ▸ In what area have I excelled as an executive? For what have I received the most praise? For what skill have I consistently gotten high marks during performance evaluations? Is that skill critical for success in my new venture?

The point of these questions is to direct you toward an entrepreneurial career for which you're qualified and that you'll enjoy. If you want to be a consultant, there's not much point if you're basically a loner who doesn't truly relish dealing with people. If you want to make loads of money with your own car-repair business, you'd better find a way to repair a whole lot of cars.

In one sense, your entrepreneurial choices are infinite. In another sense, however, they are limited—by what you enjoying doing, your skills, and your goals. Take into consideration all the issues in the preceding list and you'll choose wisely and well.

Before making your choice, examine the "entrepreneurial menu" shown in Figure 4-2, which starts on the next page. It suggests the advantages and disadvantages of various entrepreneurial possibilities, including type of business and organizational structure. As with any menu, the purpose of this one is to give you a preview of your options. Look it over and see which choices fit your particular needs and situation.

Figure 4-2. The entrepreneurial menu: Choices for the executive seeking to start a business.

Entrepreneurial Options

Consultant

Advantages	*Disadvantages*
Permits you to maximize your previous corporate contacts. Low start-up costs. Office space and staffing requirements are limited. Involves a relatively easy transition from corporate employee to entrepreneur.	Initially, somewhat dependent on corporate-related contacts. Limited earning potential. Often a one-person operation; isolation.

Spin-offs (franchises, licensing deals, distributorship)

Advantages	*Disadvantages*
Permits you to capitalize on an existing entity, using its resources, name recognition, etc. Possibility of hooking up with a hot or trendy group. Chance to dovetail your corporate skills with other resources you might not have. Low start-up costs (with the exception of certain franchise deals).	Does not provide total independence; you must maintain ties to a larger organization. Can duplicate many of the problems of being a corporate executive.

Equity arrangements (receiving partial ownership of a company as well as a salary)

Advantages	*Disadvantages*
Requires little or no financial investment. Chance to reap a financial windfall	Still involves working for someone else unless you receive more than 50

(especially if stock is part of the agreement) if the company grows. Equity deals are often struck with corporate executives by smaller companies that need their expertise.

percent ownership or options to purchase more of the company. Could be a short-term arrangement; the owners may only want you to solve a one-shot problem, or the company may view your involvement as a last resort.

Buying an existing business

Advantages

Great if you are a corporate executive who knows the industry and wants to put your knowledge to use in a smaller-scale setting. Allows you to draw on your background and bring new ideas to bear on old problems. No worries about the nitty-gritty details of starting a business from scratch; you can plunge right in and not go through the agonizing process (especially so for corporate executives) of slowly and painstakingly getting things going.

Disadvantages

You inherit other people's problems. You might feel just as trapped by the company's structure as you were when you worked for a corporation. A sizable investment is often required.

Starting from scratch

Advantages

A pure entrepreneurial venture. The complete opposite of working for a large, established organization. Freedom to shape the business in your own image. Chance for large profits.

Disadvantages

High-risk. Requires a large investment of both time and money, as well as multiple skills that you might not have acquired within the organization (especially if you were a specialist).

(continues)

Figure 4-2 (continued)

Organizational Structure

Corporation

Advantages

Structure with which ex-executives are most familiar. Provides good legal protection in the event of lawsuits. Many ex-executives find the corporate structure best for division of duties among employees and division of profits. Credit can be secured more easily than with other structures. Numerous tax benefits.

Disadvantages

Expensive to set up. Requires good record keeping, which some executives find to be a difficult and onerous task. Regulated by government agencies.

Sole proprietorship

Advantages

Easy to set up. Ideal entrepreneurial organization (far fewer restrictions than with a corporation). Meets your desire for maximum flexibility and freedom.

Disadvantages

Significant personal liability. Requires a diverse set of entrepreneurial skills that you may not have acquired within the corporation. Fewer tax benefits.

Partnership (general or limited)

Advantages

Allows risk to be spread to others. A good choice if you have specialized skills and can recruit others with complementary skills. Tax benefits (although not as many as in the past). Good structure for raising capital.

Disadvantages

Potential for problems between partners. Can involve a difficult transition if you are unaccustomed to working with others on an equal basis. Limits your freedom to control the business. Also, general partners have significant personal liability.

Type of Business

Corporate-related (a business similar to that of your former corporate employer)

Advantages	*Disadvantages*
Easier learning curve. Possibility of networking. Problems and opportunities can be assessed more quickly.	May seem too similar to your corporate job, dulling the excitement of being on your own. Feeling that you can't compete against larger companies. Difficulty of adjusting to being a small fish in a big pond.

Non-corporate-related (opening a hot-dog stand, boat marina, etc.)

Advantages	*Disadvantages*
Opportunity to leave the corporate life-style behind; dramatic change from the corporate life-style. Chance to turn a hobby or avocation into your life's work. Interacting with different types of people.	Requires more seat-of-the-pants management skills that many executives don't possess. Steep learning curve. No support group. Difficulty of making the transition from a highly structured business to a freewheeling environment.

High-risk, high-reward (restaurant, high-tech company, retail establishment, product-sales plant, etc.)

Advantages	*Disadvantages*
Possibility for sizable profits. Fast-paced, innovative, truly entrepreneurial venture. Good break if you're tired of the dull, plodding corporate environment.	Danger of "losing your shirt." Can be difficult for some executives to make such a radical transition. Requires an enormous investment of time and energy; family and social life can suffer. Entrepreneurial burnout is a consideration.

(continues)

Figure 4-2 (continued)

> **Moderate-risk, moderate-reward** (consultant, marketing-services agency, home-based business, manufacturer's representative, financial services)
>
> | *Advantages* | *Disadvantages* |
> |---|---|
> | Low start-up costs. Longer time frame in which to make the business successful. Good niche marketing opportunities. Possibility of hooking up with former corporate contacts. | Limited financial potential (at least initially). Slower pace than what you might have hoped for from an entrepreneurial business. Finding yourself too closely tied to your former corporation. |

Chapter 5
Dealing With Decisions

When executives become entrepreneurs, they find themselves faced with countless decisions. Some are big and some are small, but all are important. As a corporate manager, you were called upon to make far fewer decisions with far less personal impact. It was relatively easy to delegate minor decisions to subordinates or to postpone making major ones or to call in your peers and make decisions by committee. Now, you're the one, and often the only, decision maker. It can be an opportunity or a problem, depending on how you handle it.

Carla Bagley didn't handle it well. Carla had worked for years in the real estate acquisition department of a fast-food franchise chain. She left to open her own real estate development company. After a few months, she told me:

> I estimate I make at least forty decisions a day. Most of it is minor stuff—whom to call on the phone, should I upgrade my computer system, should I send out letter A or letter B to contacts. Then there are the major decisions, like what properties are worth pursuing, where and how I should advertise. After a while, I became paralyzed. I knew I was in trouble when I spent a whole day trying to decide on the wording of one sentence . . . and I couldn't reach a decision.

As an entrepreneur, you need an organized, methodical approach to decision making. If you don't have one, you could end up like Carla Bagley and reach the decision-saturation point. Or you could simply find yourself wasting time on decisions—time that you can't afford to waste.

To create the proper approach, divide your decisions into two categories: details and big issues. In the details category, place all the relatively minor but essential tasks: choosing a phone company, decorating the office, hiring clerical help, etc. In the big-issues category, put decisions that have a significant impact on your business's success or failure: marketing strategy, sales tactics, customer relations, etc.

Let's begin by analyzing the details list to see how you can deal most effectively with hundreds of small choices you'll be called on to make.

Sweating the Details

Most of you aren't going to be starting your business with a full staff of secretaries and subordinates to handle all the organizational details. Therefore, prepare yourself for the onslaught.

The first preparation step is to compose a list, which should include everything from setting up a bookkeeping system to compliance with various regulations to logistical matters such as garbage disposal, parking arrangements, office design, and so on. Your list will probably contain hundreds of items, but don't worry about its length. You'll find that the decision-making process becomes much more manageable once you've set the details down on paper.

Some items on the list will be no-brainers—you won't have much of a decision to make about buying office supplies, for instance. Other organizational details, however, will require a bit more thought. How many waiters does your restaurant need? Which of three different accounting software programs would best meet your requirements? Certainly, you want to give these matters due consideration. But in doing so, follow decision-making rule 1: DON'T GET BOGGED DOWN ON DETAILS.

Don't lose sight of the fact that there are larger issues that will have a much greater impact on your business. I'm sure you knew people in the corporate world who relished the minutiae—who could spend hours debating the costs and quality of one paper-clip vendor versus another. Successful entrepreneurs don't have time for such debates. Your first few months in business may be slow, however, and as you struggle to get going, you could find yourself with a lot of free time. In this case, you might be tempted to immerse yourself in details, not because you love them but because these decisions—albeit trivial—make you feel as if you're doing something. Don't waste all your available time tinkering with organizational details, though. Far better to devote that time to business planning and other activities that will impact your future revenue.

When it comes to details, you have to walk a fine line. Although spending too much time on details is an entrepreneurial sin, neither should you give them short shrift. Overlooking a crucial detail can come back to haunt you. I know of someone who opened a restaurant and failed to provide sufficient parking, violating a city zoning requirement. After the city closed him down, he recognized the importance of details. This brings us to rule 2: DON'T OVERLOOK CRUCIAL DETAILS.

As you review your list of details, you'll find that many of your choices boil down to simple versus complex. For instance, should you install a highly sophisticated accounting system or a relatively basic ledger system? Many former executives err on the side of complexity. This happens because they choose the system they used in the corporation or one recommended by a corporate buddy (who happens to be an expert in the given area).

Don't be seduced by bells and whistles, fancy price tags, or the promise of "the best." Entrepreneurs are survivors: You use only what you need. If you're a consultant, you probably require nothing more than a simple accounting system; if you're starting a factory with inventory and payables and receivables, then a more complex system is appropriate. This means you must follow rule 3: MAKE DECISIONS BASED ON REALITY NOT APPEARANCES.

A number of your decisions will involve outside advisers—lawyers, accountants, marketing-services agencies, suppliers. One of the most difficult decisions will be whether or not to follow their advice.

For instance, your lawyer tells you that you require a contract for dealings with outside parties and also specifies the sort of language that should be in the contract. He or she may draw up a ten-page contract to cover a minor project. From a legal perspective, this advice makes sense. But does it make sense from a business perspective? That's the key questions, and it's one you must ask yourself. You might decide that a ten-page contract will offend the other party; you might determine that your business would be better served by a handshake than by a legal document. Therefore, rule 4: THERE'S OFTEN A DIFFERENCE BETWEEN A SOUND LEGAL DECISION AND A SOUND BUSINESS DECISION.

This rule applies not just to legal advice but to recommendations you receive from any professional adviser. The tax strategy your accountant suggests may be based on sound accounting principles, but it may also be incompatible with the way you want to run your business.

Entrepreneurs rely on their instincts, and you should develop and rely on yours. This is probably the opposite of how you operated within the corporation. There, professional advisers offered conservative counsel, and the conservative corporation usually followed it.

Your decision on an outside consultant's advice depends, to a large extent, on what's at stake. If your lawyer insists on a ten-page contract with a number of problematic clauses and the person you're trying to sell flatly says, "I won't sign anything like this contract," then it's up to you to decide whether to sacrifice the protection the contract affords you in exchange for the business. If you're in danger of losing millions of dollars because someone refuses to sign the contract, maybe it's not worth the risk. You have to weigh the pros and cons from both a business perspective and a legal perspective.

You should bring the same attitude to intellectual-property matters: copyrights, trademarks, and patents. Copyrights are generally inexpensive and easy to procure, and if you have something uniquely yours that is of value, by all means copyright it. Trademarks are somewhat more expensive, and patents can be very costly. Besides the cost, you have to ask yourself why you're securing this protection and whether you would be willing to spend the additional money and time that might be required to defend the protection once you've bought it. Although such intellectual-property protection was standard at the corporation, the entrepreneurial business doesn't always require it—at least not in its early stages.

Where do you locate your business? Rule 5: CHOOSE A LOCATION THAT FITS YOUR BUSINESS.

Some of you may have no choice in the matter—economics dictate that you run your business out of your home. Many of you, however, will have a number of alternatives. You're going to have to decide not only where your office will be but how much space you'll need and how you'll furnish that space.

I know of a number of entrepreneurs who have erred in making these seemingly straightforward decisions. One ex-executive, who had spent her corporate life in corner offices in downtown skyscrapers, chose a prime downtown location for her consulting business. After a year of paying premium rent that left her little money for anything else, she wisely moved to more modest quarters. Another entrepreneur went the opposite route, being so concerned about his budget that he opted for dingy office space in a squalid section of the city. Unfortunately, his business, a brokerage firm, brought him well-heeled clients who were put off by the surroundings—they were reluctant to give their money to someone who appeared to be on the brink of bankruptcy.

To determine the best location for your business—as well as how to furnish the premises—ask yourself the following questions:

- *What type of location does my business demand?* For instance, if you're a retailer, you need to be in a relatively high-traffic area.
- *What are the expectations of my clients or customers?* Offices should be in keeping with those expectations. If you have a fancy office and your clients or customers expect something more modest, they may feel that their bills will reflect your rent.
- *How convenient is the location?* As I've stressed throughout this book, time is money for entrepreneurs. If your office is located far from your home or the people on whom you regularly pay calls, you'll be wasting valuable time.

▸ *What were my corporate offices like?* Many entrepreneurs try to duplicate their corporate offices on a smaller scale; it's what they're accustomed to. But if you're in a totally different business than you were as an executive—or if the size of the business is quite different—your office should reflect those differences.

The Big Issues

Unlike decisions about details, big-issue decision making draws upon a former executive's experience. Most executives have made decisions that involved millions of dollars, hundreds of people, the success of products and services. They've been called upon to decide about significant business issues. In other words, as an ex-executive, you have a clear advantage over other entrepreneurs who lack a corporate background.

Those decisions, however, affected the company, not the individual decision maker. The fact that you have now become the company fundamentally alters your decision-making process. It's one thing to risk a million dollars of the company's money; it's something else to risk a million dollars of your own.

The big-issue decisions you'll face fall into the following five categories: (1) weighing the risks, (2) rewards, (3) moral issues, (4) competition, and (5) turning points.

Weighing the Risks

For entrepreneurs, risks come in all varieties. Here are some examples:

▸ Should you borrow $100,000 or $1 million from the bank?
▸ Is it worth pursuing a major piece of new business at the expense of other smaller opportunities?
▸ Should you get involved in a project if you're not sure you have the resources to handle it?

These are the sort of risks that keep you up all night, weighing the pros and cons. They should. In many instances, the survival and prosperity of your business depend on what you decide.

Risk taking has become synonymous with entrepreneurism. Yet not all entrepreneurs take the same level of risk. I've known some who are as conservative as Swiss bankers and others who like to bet the bank with each deal. Some corporate types who become entrepreneurs believe that they're *supposed* to take huge risks, that high-level risk taking is the only way to succeed as an entrepreneur. Not so. It all depends on you and the situation you face. To help you make decisions about risk, consider the following questions.

Risk 1: Is This Something I Can Do?

Let's say you've opened a real estate business, and you're offered a deal to purchase a $25-million parcel of land in one of the hottest sections in town. In determining whether you should take the risk, you have to ask yourself, "Do I have the ability to raise the $25 million or a portion thereof and cover the interest?" In other words, can you afford to do the deal? It's not just a question of whether you can get the money but of how much of a strain it will place on you and your business. If you figure that the interest payments are only affordable if you double your business in the next year, work twice as many hours, and jeopardize everything you've built up to this point, then the risk probably isn't worth it.

Risk 2: Is My Involvement Realistic?

You round up the $25 million to purchase the land. You're all set to go when some other player in the deal—the bank, a partner, a developer, a builder, the anchor tenant for the proposed building—questions whether you're the right person for the transaction. It's a reasonable question, and one you should ask yourself.

Maybe you're not large enough to undertake this venture. Perhaps you don't have the appropriate expertise. You may be risking a great deal of money on a venture that is ill-suited to

your business. Think realistically! You're not a large corporation that can do deals of virtually any size or type. Evaluate
your resources and ascertain whether they jibe with a given
project.

Risk 3: Is This a Piece of Business I Really Want?

Suppose you can acquire the $25 million and it's a realistic
deal for your company. The next question to ask yourself is,
"Do I really want to be involved in this deal, not only now but
years down the road?"

What will the deal mean to your business in dollars and
cents? Not all business is good business. Can you make a
decent profit? Will the deal help you attract other clients? Is it
the sort of deal that will help you project the image you want?
If you're going to take a risk, make sure you have a reasonable
expectation of a payoff, both in profit and in marketing terms.
Corporations sometimes deliberately involve themselves in un-
profitable deals. They do so because they know they won't
suffer too much of a loss and will keep their people busy and
learning. You can't afford such a strategy.

Risk 4: What Is My Opportunity Cost for Taking the Risk?

By embarking on this $25-million venture, what other
opportunities might you lose? After all, this one deal will
consume your time for the next year. It will mean forsaking
three smaller opportunities that you have on the back burner.
Is the big deal worth giving up the three smaller ones? As
many entrepreneurs have told me, the best way to spread your
risk around is to have a large and diverse client base. When
you put all your eggs in one basket, you'll end up either very
rich or very poor—there's no middle ground. Furthermore, if a
project is so big that it ties up all your people and dollars, you
may not be able to go after other opportunities for a lengthy
period of time. That's risky.

Be very cautious when offered participation in ventures
that will be all-consuming. Although you might be able to

answer the first three questions in this subsection of the chapter affirmatively, if the opportunity costs seems high, beware.

Rewards

Consider risks and rewards separately. Just because you're taking the right type of risks doesn't mean you'll receive the right type of rewards. What do you want as your reward? The answer would be relatively easy if all rewards were defined solely in terms of money. But entrepreneurs can be rewarded in a number of different ways.

The first type of reward is the most obvious one: revenue. Your calculator and projections are your best tools for making decisions about this reward. Before embarking on a project, you have to estimate its profitability. If you figure you can only make $20,000, is it worth investing your time and energy?

Some entrepreneurs are like starving children: They gobble up anything that's put on their plate. Don't be so quick to take whatever is presented to you. You'll find that some projects, even if they entail little risk, offer scant financial rewards. You might be tempted to take on such a project, though, because you have nothing else to do. This is a bad idea. Another, more lucrative project might come along, and you'd have to turn it down because of your prior commitment to the barely profitable job.

There are also nonmonetary rewards. Although these have a lower priority than dollars, they should not be ignored. You'll face a number of business decisions in which there is no pot of gold at the end of your current efforts, but by saying yes, you'll create roads that lead to future gold. Ask yourself the following questions before making a decision about a major deal that may yield nonmonetary rewards:

- Is this project going to give me access to a market I'm not in now but would like to enter?
- Is it going to lead me to people who can be expected to give me additional business?
- Even if this project won't yield much short-term profit,

is this customer someone with whom I might forge a profitable long-term relationship?
▸ Will this job enhance my advertising or public relations, my image in the marketplace?
▸ Will this job improve the morale of my employees?

The final reward is personal satisfaction. For many neophyte entrepreneurs, this is a reward they can't afford. As a new entrepreneur, you will frequently be offered assignments you don't want to accept, primarily because you regard the work as dull or distasteful. You might say to yourself, "I became an entrepreneur to do what I want, and I don't want to do this." That sentiment, albeit admirable, is probably not realistic. Your first priority is to keep the business going, and that means putting the bottom line ahead of your personal likes and dislikes. Once you have the business on a solid financial footing, however, you can start placing a higher priority on personal satisfaction.

Moral Issues

Did your corporation do business with South Africa? Did it have a policy of terminating lower-level employees with little or no severance pay? Did it routinely mislead analysts about its financial health, issuing press releases that hid crucial financial data? You might not have agreed with any of these policies, but you probably kept quiet about them. You were able to separate your personal morality from the corporation's. It's far more difficult, if not impossible, to maintain that separation as an entrepreneur. You're going to face issues that force you to take a stance. Sometimes, what's good for business might be bad for your conscience. For instance, I know of an entrepreneur who intended to fire one of her employees. The employee in question was finishing up a major project, and the entrepreneur needed him to complete it because no one else had sufficient knowledge of the venture to take over. Would it be ethical to allow the man to slave away on the project— devoting a great deal of time and effort—and not inform him he was being let go until after he had completed the work? To cite another example, what happens when a prospect implies that he or she will give you a piece of business in exchange for a rebate? What if you learn that this is a regular, accepted practice in your field? Will you feel insulted that your work has been cheapened?

These types of questions have no correct answers. The only advice I can give you about such issues is that your business is a reflection of you. When it comes to ethical decisions, you have to balance practicality with your personal beliefs and find solutions you can live with.

Competition

No matter what your entrepreneurial business might be, you'll face decisions about competition. For instance:

- You open a ma-and-pa video store, and two months later, a franchise video-rental outlet opens across the street, renting videos at half the price you charge.
- You manufacture a unique toy, it does well, and everything is going along smoothly until someone knocks off your product and you lose distribution in a number of key outlets.
- Your data-processing consulting business is doing great until an accounting firm in your area creates a DP consulting arm that steals a number of your clients.

How do you respond to these competitive thrusts?

Corporations respond to competition with a variety of weapons: price cuts, advertising, promotions, new and improved products. Their responses usually require a large budget. You don't have that budget. But as an entrepreneur, you do have a number of competitive tools that big companies lack:

- *Speed:* When faced with competition, you can react far more quickly than a lumbering bureaucracy. The minute that franchise video outlet opens across the street, you can extend your hours or offer a two-for-the-price-of-one

rental special; you don't have to discuss these moves
with a committee or justify them in a ten-page report.

‣ *A distinct personality:* A large corporation is far more
impersonal than an entrepreneurial venture. Customers
or clients are attracted by you—by the way you run your
business, by your talent, by your experience. If the competition intensifies, you can decide to sell yourself
harder—spend more time tracking down leads, bring
new ideas to current clients, etc.

‣ *The ability to capitalize on your entrepreneurial status:*
Although your budget may be limited, your imagination
isn't. Instead of matching a competitor's price cut, you
might decide to add an important new service, launch a
grass-roots promotion, or come up with a way to improve your quality.

Competition will force you to make some tough decisions.
Do you match a competitor's move (at considerable expense to
you) or ignore it? Do you increase your advertising to keep up
with the business down the block?

The rule: RELY ON YOUR ENTREPRENEURIAL RESOURCES
RATHER THAN YOUR FINANCIAL ONES AND YOU'LL LEVEL THE PLAY-
ING FIELD.

Turning Points

Judy Coppel, a former corporate communications executive,
created a business that provided turnkey services for
speeches—finding speaking engagements for her clients, ghost-
writing speeches, preparing audiovisual aids, publicizing the
talks. Everyone told her it was a great idea, and her business
did well initially—her ex-employer became a client, as did four
other companies referred to her by her ex-employer. During
the first year, Judy hired two employees, and profits exceeded
her projections.

Judy entered the second year with great expectations—she
had a solid client base and assumed her business would grow
at the same rate as it had during the first year. Instead, sales
were flat, and Judy didn't know what to do. There wasn't

enough work to keep her and her employees busy. The business wasn't in danger of folding, but it didn't seem to be going anywhere, either. She had to decide: Should she maintain the status quo, fold the company, or make some changes?

Many entrepreneurs face the same decision after a relatively short time in business. Your corporate background will cause you to worry—when sales flatten out after a period of growth, this frequently signifies that the market is played out. Corporations are quick to abandon tapped-out markets, moving on to newer ones. But you, like Judy, have too much invested in your enterprise to simply "move on." Before making your decision, as yourself the following questions:

- *Was my original vision flawed?* Take a hard look at your business concept and search for weaknesses. If you find a weakness, correct it.
- *Have I given my business enough time?* If there's nothing wrong with your concept, think about the time factor. Many small enterprises grow by fits and starts, growth spurts alternating with dormant periods. It takes time to establish a niche in the marketplace—time to create widespread awareness, credibility, and contacts.
- *How are my finances?* If you've exceeded your budget, then you must decide whether you can afford to continue the business or whether you should try to raise more money. If you choose the latter option, you'll have to determine: (1) where you can obtain additional funds, (2) how much of an additional loss you can afford to sustain, and (3) what changes you can make to turn the business around.
- *Can I make changes?* Certain changes can catalyze a dormant business. You may need to run more advertising, hire a salesperson, introduce a new product or service, or fine-tune your basic concept.

Changes are critical, but many executive-entrepreneurs I've worked with have a very hard time making them. Some are paralyzed by the fact that their expected success failed to materialize: They freeze, waiting for something good to happen. Others grow depressed and become unable to do anything. Still others are reluctant to tinker with their original business concept, believing it to be perfect.

The fact is that when you started your business, you couldn't possibly have known all the issues you'd face. Once you launched it, however, you immersed yourself in the day-to-day activities and quickly learned what the real issues were. Given the benefit of that experience, you're much more perceptive about your business. Take advantage of that insight. You probably view the venture a bit differently now than when you first started. Don't be afraid to make adjustments based on what you've learned. Your company might require only minor tinkering, or it might be in need of a radical overhaul.

Making changes is not an admission of failure. It's something all good entrepreneurs do. Before deciding whether to fold your hand, take a few new cards, or stand pat, consider all your options. If you're like most former corporate managers, you'll fear the worst when your entrepreneurial business enters the doldrums—it's scary. But don't panic. Instead, first analyze the slowdown carefully, as I've suggested, then decide what to do next.

Judy Coppel, conducted such an analysis and discovered a minor flaw in her original concept. Based on a few informal discussions with corporate communications executives whom she had failed to land as clients, Judy learned that they didn't like her turnkey concept—they were under the impression (an erroneous one) that they had to purchase all or none of Judy's speech services. By tinkering with her concept—making it clear that a company was welcome to select only one or two of her services—Judy renewed her business's growth.

Chapter 6
Discipline

One of the biggest changes you'll have to deal with in the transition from executive to entrepreneur is discipline. In the corporation, discipline was external. You labored within a structure that was (depending on your corporation) relatively rigid. Your department was highly organized. There was a well-defined promotional ladder, chain of command, and stated and unstated rules and regulations. You didn't create the structure, but you did have to conform to it.

As an entrepreneur, you lack this external discipline. Suddenly, you're responsible for the structure, the timetables, the rules. The discipline is internal rather than external, and many executives find this switch difficult to make. Some are aware that they have to impose their own discipline on their ventures but don't know how to do so or where to begin. Others chafe against any type of discipline. In fleeing the corporation, they're escaping from the inflexible bureaucracy that irritated them. As one former executive told me: "I can't *wait* until I'm on my own. My company isn't going to have all the stupid, petty rules of a big corporation. I'm going to keep things loose and give everyone as much freedom as possible." Such a well-intentioned strategy often backfires, however. As entrepreneurs soon learn, people need discipline. If they don't have it, they may take advantage of their freedom to the detriment of the business.

Where does discipline start, and how do you create it? Let's begin with the most obvious issue—the discipline required to set up shop in the first place.

Finding an Entrepreneurial Business

As I conducted research among executives who became entrepreneurs, I found that a startling number of them told me how they had traveled around the country searching for a business. I was surprised not only by how many had embarked upon this journey but by how long the journey had lasted—often a year or more. It struck me that for a lot of these individuals, looking for a business had *become* their business.

After working for a corporation for years, many of these ex-executives relished the vast expanse of time opening up before them. A number of them had also received sizable termination packages, giving them the financial freedom to do whatever they wanted for a year or more. In short, they had time and money on their hands. If they were serious about becoming entrepreneurs, though, they weren't using that time and money wisely. Rather than investing in a business, they were investing in travel.

Therefore, the first disciplinary measure you should take after leaving the corporation is to set a time limit for your new-business search. If you don't, you'll end up like Moses, wandering aimlessly in an entrepreneurial desert. Although there is no ideal time limit for everyone, give yourself months rather than years.

To save yourself some time, decide what you're looking for before you embark on your journey. Define your quest by asking yourself some basic questions:

- What type of business makes my pulse race?
- What would be the ideal location?
- What is my goal for my business (millions of dollars versus an income equal to that earned as an executive, an industry leadership position versus moderate profitability)?
- What is a realistic business for me (in terms of my resources, abilities, and money)?

Here's a rule of thumb to keep in mind while you're searching: The longer you wait before starting your business, the less likely it is that you'll ever start it. A lengthy delay often gives rise to second thoughts; it can drain your financial resources; during this interim period, you may receive a job offer from another corporation—an offer too good to refuse. If you truly want to be an entrepreneur, discipline yourself so you can become one.

Initial Distractions

As soon as you leave the corporation, a virtually endless list of distractions will take your eye off your entrepreneurial goal. Everything you've postponed because of the demands of work will suddenly seize your attention: repairs on the house, family commitments, organizing the boxes of stuff you brought home from the office. If you let it, such busywork can become all-consuming.

It's easy to get sidetracked by distractions. As a corporate employee, you were conditioned to do things based on other people's priorities. A boss would invariably ask you, "Is it done yet?" You accomplished tasks because you were accountable to others for their completion. Now, you're accountable only to yourself. As a result, you procrastinate. Often, mowing the lawn seems more appealing than struggling with a new business plan. It can be especially appealing if you're suffering from what I call "the ex-executive syndrome."

What Ifs

Victims of the ex-executive syndrome constantly ask themselves a series of "what if" questions, replaying what went wrong and what they might have done differently. This is especially true if your departure was instigated by others. The result: You can't concentrate on your entrepreneurial aspirations because you're so caught up in the emotional wake of leaving the organization.

Consider the following statements, which are typical of people afflicted by this syndrome:

- Maybe I should have left the organization years ago when ABC Corporation offered me that job.
- If only I could have achieved that last sales objective I wouldn't have been terminated.

> ▸ If I had accepted the transfer, I might still be with the company.
> ▸ Perhaps I deserved to be fired; after all, I messed up my boss's pet project.

All these "what ifs" drain your emotional energy—energy you should be investing in your business. If you become obsessed with paths not taken and mistakes made, you'll never marshal the inner resources every entrepreneur needs.

Discipline yourself. There's nothing you can do about the past, so put it behind you. Adopt the attitude that "it doesn't matter how I got here." You're here and you have to move on. Concentrate on the present and the future. The more focused you are on your new business, the more likely you'll be to get it off the ground.

The Fear of Failure

As soon as your entrepreneurial dream is on the brink of reality—you're about to sign a bank loan or open your place of business—the fear of failure looms. This is especially likely to happen if you were terminated from your corporate job. You worry that you'll fail again, that the corporation eliminated you because you don't really have what it takes to succeed.

Or it might be that you fear being an entrepreneur. When you were a corporate executive and dreamed of running your own business, there was no fear because your dream seemed at best a distant, hypothetical prospect. But now that it's actually about to happen, you start second-guessing yourself. You think of all the unknowns and become a fish out of water: A corporate executive you always were, a corporate executive you'll always be. If you try to be something you're not, you're doomed to fail.

In either instance, the specter of failure can paralyze you. It can lead to postponing the decision to "do it" and instead spending additional months procrastinating—conducting research, traveling, writing elaborate plans.

I know of one entrepreneur who delayed opening his business for two years after leaving his organization. Once he departed, he worked diligently to set up his venture—an antiques store. He arranged the financing, found a great location (signing a lease for the space), created a business and financial plan, spent time at flea markets and estate sales buying merchandise (which he stored in his basement and garage). But he couldn't take the final step: opening his doors for business. Here's how he explained his hesitation:

> I was scared. When I left my company after eight years, it was unpleasant. My boss said I was let go because my productivity had declined; he told me that of the five people in my group, I was number five. When I decided to open my antiques store, my coworkers were supportive; they all said how envious they were, that they were sure I'd do great. I thought so, too, until the time came to actually do it. Then, this little voice in my head started whispering: "What makes you think you can be an entrepreneur; think about how disappointed all your coworkers will be when the business doesn't work; your boss will laugh and say, 'I told you so.'" That little voice became a big problem.

To overcome this problem, discipline your failure-avoidance tendencies. You can acquire such discipline by telling yourself two things—and really believing them:

1. *History won't repeat itself.* If you failed at the corporation, it doesn't follow that you'll fail in your own business. I've found no correlation between the two. In fact, many successful entrepreneurs were fired by their corporation.
2. *My entrepreneurial endeavor is what I want, and I'm going to do everything to make it work; I won't just go through the motions.* Think positive! Discipline yourself to accept failure as a possibility, not a probability. Without that discipline, you'll take halfhearted steps and never get your venture off the ground.

Reaffirming Your Identity

Executives who become entrepreneurs leave part of themselves behind. Like police officers who become private detectives, they give up their uniform.

Your identity was wrapped up in your position within the corporation. Your office, status, title, pay and perks, duties, boss, subordinates—everything contributed to the way you perceived yourself and were perceived by others. As a corporate executive, you automatically received a measure of respect, authority, and acceptance. When you turned into an entrepreneur, all that disappeared. Without your corporate position, you may feel identityless, like a shell of your former self. You may start doubting your judgment and questioning your own authority for doing anything.

Although it's a natural reaction, it's also illusory. You haven't changed; your environment has. Entrepreneurs require self-confidence, ego, and aggressiveness. If you had those qualities as an executive, you'll have them as an entrepreneur. Trust your instincts and abilities.

Setting Priorities

Entrepreneurial discipline also involves focusing on what's crucial to the business's survival and profitability. As an executive, you may have agonized for hours over the wording of a letter before releasing it; you may have spent weeks or months developing systems that would allow your department to operate at maximum efficiency.

As an entrepreneur, your priorities change, especially in the initial stages of the business. Your top priority is survival, and that means refusing to allow less pressing issues to distract you. It might be easier and more enjoyable to create promotions for the next quarter or to map out long-range strategies on your computer. Survival issues are often unpleasant: If you don't increase next month's revenue by 25 percent, should you fire your assistant? If your major client cuts back on his or her orders, how can you line up another client within the next three weeks?

To discipline yourself to deal with these survival issues, answer the following questions. But don't just answer them once and then forget about them. Review them periodically:

- ▸ Is what I'm doing going to have an immediate effect on the success of my business?
- ▸ Is what I'm doing going to result in a sale or the generation of revenue?
- ▸ Did I come up with ways to reduce expenses?
- ▸ Did I find a way to enter new markets?
- ▸ Will what I've done today affect my business today, tomorrow, next week, or next month?
- ▸ Is there something I should be doing that will affect my business's survivability and profitability?
- ▸ Is my business in danger of failing?
- ▸ Is what I'm doing right now going to lessen that danger?

These are entrepreneurial—not executive—questions. They have a great deal to do with the discipline you impose on your time and resources. As an entrepreneur, you're going to face a mind-boggling variety of choices involving your time and resources. Always choose what's most important to your business, not what seems the most fun or easiest.

In addition, you'll find that you have a series of projects that only you can handle. You can't delegate them to anyone else. Accept the fact that many of these projects are never going to get done—or at best, that it will be a long time before you do them. Prioritize your projects; then concentrate on the ones that directly affect your survival and put the others on the back burner.

Disciplining Yourself and Others

Think about what it would have been like when you were a corporate executive if one day your secretary, subordinates, computer, and various other resources had been taken away from you. Your work life would have been a mess. Because your discipline was external rather than internal, you didn't have the structure and controls necessary to establish a productive, smoothly functioning system.

When you begin your entrepreneurial venture, you'll be faced with a similar situation. As one neophyte entrepreneur told me, "When I started my business, my biggest worry was how I would organize everything myself. At my former company, I would have been lost without my staff. I was hopelessly disorganized."

I told this entrepreneur about my son. When he lived at home, his room was always a mess. When he went to college and I visited him for the first time, I expected his room to be in similar disarray. Instead, it was neat as a pin. I asked him what accounted for the change. He replied, "The room at home was yours. This one is mine."

As an entrepreneur, the business is yours. This will have a positive effect on your approach to such issues as organization and structure. You'll find yourself being much more careful about how you portion out your time, your schedule, your methods of doing business. No matter how undisciplined you might have been as a corporate executive, you'll probably have a natural impetus to be more organized once you're on your own.

There are really two issues here: discipline you impose on yourself and discipline you impose on people who work for you. Don't assume they're the same thing.

To create discipline for yourself, think about the structure that suits you best. Don't follow the structure suggested in a book or duplicate your former company's structure. Think about an environment in which you'll operate at peak efficiency. If you tend to be most productive in the morning, schedule yourself accordingly.

What suits you, however, might not suit your employees. Although you may enjoy a loose, open environment, you may find that your people are unproductive in such a setting. Therefore, create some rules addressing the following structural issues:

- Work hours
- Compensation schedules

- Reporting (who reports to whom and how often)
- Personnel-review procedures and policies
- Timetables
- Budgets (keeping track of expenditures and authorization for expenditures)

One of the great advantages you have over entrepreneurs without corporate experience is that you've been exposed to all these structures. Capitalize on what you know and implement a structure that makes sense to you and your employees.

Crucial to this process is establishing a method to enable you to determine whether something was done, and done right. If you have a restaurant, you must set up a system to ensure that the freshest fish is purchased from the right supplier and that it is then stored and prepared properly. As the restaurant owner, you probably can't be directly involved with all these functions. You have to reply on buyers, vendors, chefs, and other employees. With a good system in place, though, you can increase the odds of all these jobs' being carried out efficiently.

The bottom line is that discipline ensures accountability, not only on your part, but on the part of others upon whom the success of your business depends.

Chapter 7

Traps

Every entrepreneur faces traps. They come with the territory. By definition, entrepreneurs have a tremendous amount of freedom; they aren't shackled by bosses or boards of directors or shareholders. The flip side of this freedom is that there's no one to say, "You might want to think twice" or "I'd check that deal more carefully before buying into it."

For the former corporate executive, entrepreneurial traps are numerous. Although your corporate background gives you many advantages as an entrepreneur, it also makes you vulnerable to many pitfalls. No matter how entrepreneurial you may be, you can't eliminate your corporate mind-set overnight. Whether consciously or unconsciously, you'll be prey to the traps it sets.

What are those traps, and how can they be overcome? This chapter should help you identify them and extricate yourself should you become ensnared.

Trap 1: Abusing and Misusing Your Resources

A businessperson has three major resources: time, money, and expertise. Although, at your former organization, your supply of these resources may not have been unlimited, it *was* plentiful. More important, most of these resources weren't yours. Because they were corporate resources, they were virtually inexhaustible. To achieve the ends of an approved, budgeted project, you could tap a variety of resources without fear of the well's running dry. As an entrepreneur, on the other hand, the majority of resources are your own. If you squander time, money, or expertise, your business will suffer.

Resource management is critical, and it's not as easy as it

sounds. I've seen many entrepreneurs overestimate their resources. The $100,000 bank loan they've received seems as if it will go a long way. Freed of onerous, bureaucratic tasks, former executives feel as if they have all the time in the world. Their expertise is also boundless: What they don't know, they'll learn. In reality, however, neophyte entrepreneurs are constantly strapped for cash, time, and expert assistance. Former executives find it hard to "buy cheap"—to pinch pennies in order to maintain a business-sustaining cash flow. The concept of trade-offs—choosing between a computer system and a secretary—is foreign to them. Going from corporate prince to entrepreneurial pauper involves a tremendous psychological adjustment.

Similarly, ex-executives struggle with decisions to hire "outsiders"—lawyers, accountants, computer specialists, financial planners, management and marketing consultants. Not only is it costly, but these experts are outside the loop. Functions that executives once assigned to trusted subordinates must now be delegated to people with no vested interest in the entrepreneurial venture.

Time management is perhaps the most insidious trap. Many executive-entrepreneurs spend an excessive amount of time planning, preparing, and testing. They want to make sure everything is perfect, so they build models of their business, subjecting them to cost analysis and feasibility studies. Unfortunately, entrepreneurs don't usually have this luxury. Although this was proper form at the corporation, it's unacceptable for a small, new business. Windows of opportunity close quickly, and entrepreneurs who try to finesse every detail will watch as opportunities pass them by.

To avoid abusing or misusing your resources, take the following steps:

‣ Budget your available dollars for reality, not appearances; give priority to the expenditures that will help you survive, not to the ones that will merely improve your business's image or provide greater convenience.
‣ Don't spend money to "oversophisticate" your business—fancy business cards; stationery; brochures; beau-

tiful, high-rent offices; first-class travel and entertainment. Although these frills might boost your venture's image, they aren't as important as ensuring its survival. Choose the expenditures that really make a difference.

▸ Strike a balance between hiring outside help and doing the work yourself. If you try to do it all, you'll be spending too much time on things you're not good at or don't care about doing well. If you hire outsiders to do too much, you'll run up a sizable bill and endanger the business. Identify your strengths and weaknesses and concentrate on strength-oriented tasks.

▸ Don't sweat the small stuff. Too much planning and not enough action has destroyed more than one promising entrepreneurial endeavor.

Trap 2: Mistake Mania

As an executive, the mistakes you made were relatively easy to hide or live with. Unless you were the marketing person who dreamed up New Coke, you probably didn't suffer directly if you exceeded your budget or submitted a flawed plan. The worst thing that probably happened was your boss's chewing you out. As an entrepreneur, in contrast, your mistakes have immediate, visible consequences. Poor budgeting might mean being unable to meet a payroll. Shipping the wrong product might cause an account to terminate its relationship with you. You might spend a hefty sum on a direct-mail campaign and not receive a single response.

Both large companies and small entrepreneurial businesses make mistakes. The former, however, can keep their mistakes private. (I'm sure you can recall a number of blunders made by your former organization; I'm also sure that few, if any, became known to the outside world.) The trick is not to become consumed by your mistakes, because it's not the mistakes themselves that can devastate a new entrepreneurial venture; it's the entrepreneur's reaction to those mistakes. I know of one man, a few months into his computer-systems business, whose first big sale fell through when his cost estimate turned out to be $30,000 less than the actual price. He chastised himself unmercifully, eventually folding the business.

Accept your mistakes and resign yourself to the fact that you'll make most of them during the first year. Few mistakes will put you out of business. At worst, they'll be temporary setbacks. Rejoice that you no longer have to rationalize or hide them. One of the reasons you became an entrepreneur was to have the opportunity to take calculated risks. Obviously, not all of them will pan out. Don't overreact and try to make every project mistakeproof.

Trap 3: Hiring the Wrong People the Wrong Way

Most of you won't regard hiring as a trap. After all, you've hired scores of people in the past; you have a good track record of bringing in talented managers for demanding positions. How difficult could it be to hire a few people for your start-up business?

Before you answer, talk to other executives about their first hires as entrepreneurs. They'll tell you horror story after horror story. I know of one former merchandising manager who opened a clothing store and ran through six store managers during her first year. Here's how she described the problem:

> I thought I was pretty good at spotting the right people for jobs; at my former employer, I can't recall one hiring mistake I made. When I opened my store, though, I hired people who just didn't fit in—each one seemed to be worse than the one before. In retrospect, all I can think is that while I was great a hiring employees for others, I was terrible at hiring them for myself.

Her problem is typical. Among the hiring mistakes former executives frequently make are:

- ▸ Hiring the first person who walks through your door. You're desperate for somebody, anybody (especially if

somebody/anybody is a salesperson), and feel you can't
afford to wait until exactly the right person comes along.

‣ Hiring someone who is right for the job but wrong for
you. At the corporation, you were able to get along with
any subordinate, as long as he or she produced. In a
small business, it's much more difficult to get along with
someone if that individual is the only other person in
your office.

‣ Hiring an employee who is ill-equipped to deal with the
stresses inherent in any small, start-up business. The
person you hire might be well-qualified for the position
but never have participated in an entrepreneurial venture before. Perhaps this individual, like you, comes from
a large corporation but, unlike you, can't tolerate the
risks and the day-to-day crises.

These traps can be avoided, but only if you acknowledge that
the entrepreneurial hiring process is different from the corporate one.

The most obvious difference is that prospective employees
don't come to you prescreened. At the corporation, your human
resources department separated the wheat from the chaff,
making sure not only that job candidates were qualified for the
position but that they were compatible with the corporate
culture. A large organization's culture is a reflection of thousands of employees, whereas your culture is you—your personality and values. During your interviews, pay close attention to
each applicant's personality and values. If they clash with
yours, he or she probably won't fit in.

The second way in which the entrepreneurial hiring process differs from the corporate one is that you don't automatically begin the process with a want ad. Unless you have human
resources skills, you'll want to prequalify candidates. There
are two ways to do this. The first involves an executive search
organization. This type of service is great if you can afford it
and if you have a relatively high-level position to fill. Most of
you, however, will be strapped for cash, and since the fee will
be 15 percent to 30 percent of the employee's first-year salary,
you may want to choose the second option: networking. Talk to

friends and former coworkers; request names of people who might be right for the job. Because your coworkers and friends know you, and will take your personality and needs into account before submitting names, you'll get better-quality candidates from them than from a want ad.

Third, be careful of applicants whose previous experience is solely corporate. Moving from an organization with two thousand employees to one with two people is a jolt. You might be able to make that transition, but someone who is not a business owner or who lacks an entrepreneurial mind-set might not. More than one entrepreneur has invested time and money to train an employee, only to find the person gone after a few months. To gauge a job candidate's adaptability to your environment, ask the following questions:

- ▸ What did you dislike about working for a large corporation?
- ▸ Do you have any misgivings about working for a small business?
- ▸ What is your greatest fear about this job?
- ▸ What is your career goal? If you could have your choice of any job, what would it be?

Although there are no correct answers to these questions, there *are* incorrect ones—at least from an entrepreneurial perspective. If, for instance, someone says that his or her greatest fear is that the job will be too pressure-laden and there won't be sufficient resources, it's a clear indication that this person is not the one to hire. Think about the way you'd answer the questions and see how close each applicant comes to your responses.

Trap 4: Bringing In a Partner

Being on your own is difficult. It's especially difficult after years of working as part of a team. When you first leave the corporation, you might relish the thought of independence. But a few months into your entrepreneurial venture, you might have second thoughts. You might say to yourself, "Gee, it would be great to have someone to bounce ideas off of, to share the risk, to do the things I can't." You start looking for a partner.

Partnerships aren't necessarily bad. They offer a variety of benefits and shouldn't be dismissed out of hand. But they should be entered into with caution. Small-business partnerships can end up like broken marriages: The custody battles (in this case, for the business) can be costly and destructive.

One of the most common partnership problems occurs when the entrepreneur is looking to hire somebody for a key position and finds a person who seems like the ideal candidate. The hitch is that this individual wants more money than the entrepreneur can pay, so the entrepreneur decides to offer him or her a piece of the business—maybe not 50 percent, but a significant percentage.

In most cases, I've found this arrangement to be a mistake. No matter how much your new partner contributes, he or she won't contribute as much as you do. Ask yourself the following: "Will this person bring as much passion and energy and talent to the business as I have? Will he or she bring even a fraction of what I've brought?" Consider the fact that your other employees—who weren't offered a partnership—may resent your willingness to give a piece of the business to an outsider.

Another crucial issue is money. You've put a significant amount of money into your business. Your partner hasn't put in one cent. If the business fails, you won't be able to walk away with as much as you could have sans partner. Many entrepreneurs grow to resent this situation, even if the business does well. You've offered your new partner the opportunity to ride the business's upside without assuming any downside risk.

Finally, your new partner is capitalizing on your idea. No matter how valuable this person becomes, he or she still wasn't there at the beginning and is taking advantage of your concept without compensating you for your initial spadework.

The following "don't" rules will help you decide whether to bring in a partner:

> ▸ Don't bring in anyone who won't put some of his or her money into the business.

▶ Don't bring in a partner merely because you want some-body to use as a sounding board.
▶ Don't offer a partnership as a hiring incentive.
▶ Don't offer a partnership to someone who won't make equal (or near-equal) contributions in terms of money, time, energy, talent, and ideas.

These are two valid reasons for establishing a partnership: (1) You need your partner's money to launch or sustain the business; (2) he or she helped you formulate the business concept and possesses necessary skills that you lack. If neither of these reasons applies to your situation, be wary of partners.

Trap 5: Losing Objectivity

Veteran entrepreneurs develop a jaundiced eye for great, can't-miss ideas. They've been through the start-up process too many times and witnessed too many failures to view them any other way. Executives, though bring a different perspective to their new ventures. More often than not, great ideas imple-mented through corporate pathways work; or at the very least, they don't bomb. Corporations have the financial resources, clout, and skills to give a great idea a good chance of succeed-ing. The process itself—for example, committees, market re-search—will weed out bad ideas.

If you're like many executive-entrepreneurs, you'll leave the corporation burning to bring your great idea to market. You'll be wildly enthusiastic about it. Friends will tell you it's going to make you rich. Such enthusiasm is useful. But it can also be a trap. A friend of mine started a business with all the potential in the world. It was a service that helped injured and lost children receive assistance quickly and effectively. Every-thing suggested that my friend's service would be successful. The timing was right, as was the market demand. Everyone told him it was the greatest idea since sliced bread. But the service failed, and failed fast. No one was sure why it failed, except for the fact that it was hard to sell. My friend couldn't believe it. He'd invested considerable time and money in his new business and was shocked when it didn't take off.

He shouldn't have been. Great new ideas that have never been tried before are dangerous for beginning entrepreneurs. They assume that the idea is so fresh and unique, it's bound to work. They won't have any competition. Nothing, they assume, can stand in the way of a great new idea.

Nothing, that is, except the idea itself. Consider that there might be a reason why something has never been done before. New ideas are the hardest ones to sell, especially for neophyte entrepreneurs. Not only are you starting from scratch, but you're starting with a product or service with which the market is unfamiliar.

Entrepreneurs thrive on new, untested ideas, so don't dismiss them out of hand. Then again, recognize the potential traps if your business depends on such an idea. The following subsections present four ways to avoid falling victim to the "objectivity" trap.

Education

Selling is an educational process, and you're going to have a tough time educating your market about your new product or service. Before buying, prospective customers ask, "Is this something I'm familiar and comfortable with?"

Finances

Because educating the market takes time, it will also take significant amounts of money. Do you have enough funds to make it through the eduational period? It might be months or even years before the awareness and acceptance levels are high enough to generate sufficient revenue. If you're in this situation, your marketing is critical. Determine what media you'll need to advertise in to communicate your message—how much your media expenditures will be, how much you'll have to pay for the production of ads, how often your ads will have to run to do the job, and so on. Figure out the ideal marketing budget and decide whether you have the funds for it.

Resources

You could have a great idea but be the wrong person to implement it. You might lack not only the financial resources but the skills, people, and contacts necessary to make it work. Certainly, you can gather those resources over time. But if the time to implement the idea is now, you don't have that luxury. For example, an inventor can come up with the formula for a new, fuel-saving gasoline, but only a large oil company can successfully market such a product.

Credibility

For someone starting a new business, the hardest job is establishing credibility. It's difficult if not impossible to gain instant credibility. It's a gradual process, and you have to work night and day for a long time to convince key people inside and outside your industry that you're a legitimate player.

Therefore, you might possess a great idea and all the resources in the world but still lack "brand acceptance." Your company's name is meaningless. You've created a wonderful new food product, but the chain stores won't carry it because you're a nobody; shelf space is tight, and they're not going to drop a General Foods product to squeeze yours in.

Given time, money, and resources, you can overcome all these obstacles. You may well have that rare great idea that is so timely and powerful that it sweeps all obstacles aside. Thousands of small companies have made their great ideas pay off through persistence and hard work. (Apple Computer, if you recall, began in a garage.) But many companies fail because they are overly reliant on the strength of their great ideas, especially when those ideas are so new and unusual that the market has no frame of reference for them.

If you feel you're falling into this trap, consider an alternative: Sell or license your idea to a larger organization. Capitalize on its resources and credibility. A large company might be willing to market your product or give you access to its distribution network. But doesn't this violate the entrepreneurial spirit? Not necessarily. You may be able to exist as a relatively independent subsidiary of a larger organization. You might find that you enjoy a comfortably hybrid status: half-entrepreneur, half–corporate executive. Or you might be able to use the proceeds from the sale of your idea to fund a new, different entrepreneurial business.

Whatever your decision, beware of losing your objectivity. No matter how many people tell you that your business idea is terrific, don't take their word for it. Analyze it carefully before proceeding.

Trap 6: The China-Egg Syndrome

Corporate managers are generally excellent salespeople. They've developed experience and expertise in selling to their bosses, their subordinates, their outside resources, their markets. In large meetings and one-on-one settings, they've sold everything from concepts to programs to policies. The only thing they haven't sold is a product or service for their own, personal profit. That kind of sale, of course, is what entrepreneurial selling is all about.

Entrepreneurs fall into a trap when they fail to recognize that this is a different type of selling. The best example of this sort of trap is the china-egg syndrome. You've just started your business, and you begin calling on prospective customers. One prospect seems as if he's going to buy; he tells you how much he likes what you're selling, how valuable he thinks your product or service will be. But he doesn't sign on the dotted line. Still, you recognize that Rome wasn't built in a day—you're sure that he'll buy eventually. So you continue to visit the prospect, leaving his office each time thinking that one more visit will clinch the sale. But it won't. The prospect is a china egg—no matter how long you sit on it, it won't hatch.

Your selling persistence might have worked at the corporation. There, through your own efforts, you could have exerted enough pressure to get your agenda adopted. But selling a product or service is another ball game. You have to realize when you've struck out, even if your internal scoreboard says the count is even. The first rule of entrepreneurial selling, then, is: DIFFERENTIATE BETWEEN THE CHINA EGGS AND THE LIVE ONES. To entrepreneurs, time is money, and you can't afford to waste any. If you do, you'll miss out on other prospects who are worth pursuing.

Another common mistake for executive-entrepreneurs is to overtarget their markets. *Target marketing* is a buzzword in corporate America, and for good reason. The logic of concentrating on the 25 percent of a market that will account for 85 percent of your sales is unassailable. An entrepreneur who targets too tightly, however, will miss the mark. The more prospects you hit, the greater your chances of making a sale. So the second rule of entrepreneurial selling is: HIT AS MANY PROSPECTS AS YOU CAN. This might seem self-evident, but I've known many entrepreneurs who have concentrated all their efforts on a handful of prospects. If you try this strategy and your prospects don't pan out, you're back to square one.

Another trap for executive-entrepreneurs is a short-term mentality. The corporation, with its emphasis on quarterly earnings, fosters this mind-set, making it hard to look beyond the current quarter. Translated to a selling environment, that means focusing on short-term sales. Selling something to a customer once is good; selling something to a customer ten times is much better. Thus, you want to establish long-term customer relationships—the kind that will give your business a foundation on which to build. You can only establish long-term relationships by identifying your customers' real concerns and needs. If you concentrate exclusively on making the sale, you won't achieve that objective. You'll have to probe and listen and respond to the customers' needs. If you can successfully communicate that your product or service will meet those needs, you'll have made a repeat customer. Therefore, the third rule of entrepreneurial selling is: FOCUS ON LONG-TERM CUSTOMER RELATIONSHIPS.

Another selling trap is dealing with non–decision makers. Don't expect to make sales to the decision maker's subordinates. It doesn't happen. When you schedule your appointments, arrange to see the people in power. Otherwise, you'll receive responses like, "I can't do anything until I talk to my boss." More often than not, that translates into a no-sale.

Hence, the fourth rule of entrepreneurial selling: DEAL WITH THE DECISION MAKERS.

Finally, enter sales situations confidently and positively. Many executives who become entrepreneurs find that difficult. They were used to dealing with outsiders from a position of power. Now that they are entrepreneurs, the situation is reversed. Without the corporation's protection, they go into selling situations with hat-in-hand, intimidated by their lack of power.

Although selling often takes place in a negative environment, don't let it get to you. Unlike other entrepreneurs, you have a track record with a major corporation. Prospects will be impressed with your credentials and perceive you differently than someone who has always been on his or her own. You might be a neophyte entrepreneur, but you're not a neophyte businessperson. Therefore, don't enter a prospect's office as if you're asking for a favor. Communicate your belief that you have something of value to offer, that your product or service will be of great importance to the prospect's business. The more confident and credible you are, the better your chances of making the sale. That's why the fifth rule of entrepreneurial selling is: SELL FROM STRENGTH, NOT WEAKNESS.

Trap 7: Becoming Spoiled by Success

Your new business takes off. Money is rolling in; the phone is ringing off the hook. You're on top of the world. It's a great feeling, one experienced by every executive who successfully makes the transition to entrepreneur.

Don't let success go to your head, though. No one is invulnerable. And no one is more vulnerable than nouveaux riches entrepreneurs. If you're one of the lucky ones—everything you do during the first year seems to come up roses—you may well think you can do no wrong. It's a natural reaction. After all, you haven't done anything wrong so far.

But remember that entrepreneurship is synonymous with risk. What goes up must come down. Newspaper business sections are filled with stories of entrepreneurs who bit off more than they chould chew, who overextended themselves and ended up in bankruptcy court.

Your initial success is probably the result of a number of factors: your great idea, your timing, your luck, your contacts. One or all of those factors can turn against you. Markets dry up, competitors steal your customers, a business concept becomes outmoded. The point is, Don't become overconfident. Take calculated risks. Don't wager more money than you can afford to lose. Avoid worst-case scenarios.

One of the reasons you became an entrepreneur was the freedom it offered. It's great to take advantage of that freedom through new ventures, expansion, and testing innovative concepts. Keep doing so. But don't get yourself in a position where one failure could put you out of business. Somewhere down the road, you'll experience failure. You'll survive that failure if you refuse to bet the bank on every new deal.

THREE

Cases in Point

The four chapters in Part Three present situations and advice specific to your particular entrepreneurial activity. Chapters 8, 9, and 10 discuss the most common types of entrepreneurial ventures: consulting, retailing, and product sales. In each chapter, I've provided examples of people who have made the transition from executive to entrepreneur—a division vice-president who became a consultant, for instance.

One way to approach these chapters would be to zero in on the one that is relevant to your particular entrepreneurial venture and read it carefully. By learning about the mistakes and successes of others, you can increase your odds of minimizing the former and maximizing the latter. However, I think you might find it instructive to read all three of these chapters. Even though two of them may deal with a type of entrepreneurial activity other than the one you have chosen, many of the problems and opportunities faced by executive-entrepreneurs overlap, so you should find something of value in each chapter.

Chapter 11 deals with special situations. If your venture doesn't fit neatly into the aforementioned categories, the material here is for you. Perhaps you're an "unretired" executive starting a second career, or you've decided to turn a lifelong hobby into a business. The chapter covers these and other special situations in detail.

Chapter 8

Consulting

Consulting often appears to be the easiest route to entrepreneurship for a corporate executive. It's a relatively inexpensive option, and it frequently draws on the executive's expertise. If you're considering opening a consulting business, however, you should know that the consulting environment can be stifling for certain executives. In many ways, it is further removed from a corporate job than any other type of entrepreneurial endeavor.

In gathering information for this chapter, I talked to numerous executive-consultants, some of whom succeeded and some of whom failed. Rather than document all their stories, I'll begin by focusing on one consultant whose experiences and observations strike me as "typical"—in the sense that he went through a process many of you will go through if you choose to start a consulting firm business.

From Food-Service Executive to Consultant

For a long time, John Seastone was a satisfied, productive, and high-ranking employee of the Walgreen Company. He'd worked for the company for twenty-five years, rising through the ranks to become vice-president in charge of the Wags food-service division. During that time, he gave little thought to becoming an entrepreneur; he loved his job. Then, things began to change.

Leaving After Twenty-Five Years

In 1988, Walgreen's was sold to Marriott, and it looked as if John would have to relocate. At age 55, with most of his family in the Chicago area, he had no desire to move, so he resigned. He left Walgreen's with substantial benefits—enough so that he didn't have pressing financial concerns. But John was too young to retire. Initially, he searched for another corporate job in the food-service field. Although he would have enjoyed joining an organization similar to Wags, the opportunities in Chicago were scarce—the type of organizations he was interested in were located elsewhere.

Working with an outplacement firm, John soon realized that he needed to explore other alternatives. When the firm suggested consulting, John wasn't particularly interested. It wasn't that he disliked the idea of consulting. It was simply that corporate life was all he knew, he liked the corporate work style, and he'd been highly successful at it. But the phone started ringing when John left Wags—people had seen the announcement of his resignation in the trade papers and were anxious to solicit his help. He was the type of high-profile executive who invariably attracts consulting assignments.

Still, John balked. He kept asking himself, "What if I fail?" He said to himself, "I worried that I'd do a job and it wouldn't work out, and that they would say, 'Don't call Seastone; he's terrible.' That really bothered me." John was also bothered by the prospect of "going from the top to the bottom." As head of his division, John had been accustomed to having enormous corporate resources at his disposal. As a consultant, he would have none of those resources. John wasn't sure how he would handle it, especially at his age. "Maybe if I was younger, I wouldn't have felt this way," he said. "But I was 55. I felt a consulting career would be like starting over."

Testing the Water

John responded to a few of the companies that called him. He hadn't officially opened a consulting business, but consulting was what he was doing. The initial projects went well; most of his clients appreciated his advice and paid him accordingly. Then he began some informal networking, letting it be known that he was available for assignments. John found that he was comfortable with the work, that he could talk the language.

Gradually, his mind-set changed. As John observed, "I went from holding the corporate security blanket to realizing I didn't need it."

Finally, John decided to give consulting a fair shot. He set up an office in his home, created some marketing materials, and actively networked. He also decided to focus his consulting on the area with which he had the most experience: midpriced, family-style restaurants. "I had received calls from companies outside of my area of expertise—fast-food chains and higher-priced restaurant organizations. But I decided to concentrate on what I know best."

Wags vs. Consulting: Likes and Dislikes

John found he liked a number of things about consulting, including not being committed to a schedule. He enjoyed the flexibility—not having to worry about taking an afternoon off for golf because it would set a bad example. He also discovered that consulting involved less pressure than corporate work: "There was the constant demand to make your budget at the company, to increase sales and profits, to control expenses, to make better deals. I sure don't miss having to beat people over the head to achieve objectives." Finally, John appreciated the diversity of his assignments, ranging from analysis of how a restaurant was running to customer surveys of pricing, portions, and training programs.

On the negative side, John felt isolated, remembering that at Wags, it was rare for him to be alone for even an hour. Now, he said, he spends most of his time by himself. Another problem—one of the most ticklish John encountered—was setting his fee. At first, his friends told him to charge a high, daily fee; they insisted that his extensive experience in the business, combined with his reputation, entitled him to a premium rate. John, however, was reluctant to charge such a steep fee, primarily because some of his clients were not extremely profitable—he assumed they would be turned off by what they would consider an exorbitant fee. When he lost a few jobs because of his daily rate, John lowered it. But he still isn't sure his fee is right and is struggling to arrive at a happy medium.

The thing John disliked most about consulting was the lack of opportunity for implementation. John rhapsodized about seeing projects through from start to finish at Wags. He talked glowingly of taking a project from idea stage to completion, marshaling and integrating the company's vast resources to achieve a measurable objective. "Now, I have to be content with a piece of paper," he said. "You get paid a fee for your recommendations, not based on the performance of your recommendations. It's not the same as knowing: 'By God, this worked!' "

Lessons Learned

As of this writing, John Seastone has been a consultant for about eighteen months. He can see himself continuing his present business until he retires. But he's learned some hard lessons along the way—lessons that he's happy to pass on to other would-be consultants.

1. John emphasized the importance of "going with the flow." He said he found that he had to leave his hard-driving, demanding corporate persona behind. As an example, he related the problems he encountered on his first consulting assignments. He'd charge in with aggressive concepts, suggesting dramatic and exciting changes, only to be met by resistance.

> I learned there was no sense in making a recommendation when you know the person isn't interested in making that type of change. You have to take it slow, find out what makes your client tick, his concerns and values. Once you learn the direction he's coming from, you can ease into your recommendation and make it acceptable.

2. John discovered that he had to change the image he presented to clients. His button-down shirts, strongly held opinions, and luxury car created the wrong impression: "I could see smaller clients wondering, 'What's this slicker going

to try and sell us?' " John gradually modified his approach, favoring a sportscoat and loafers rather than pinstripes and wing tips; he also learned to park his luxury car out of sight of first-time clients. He listened more and talked less, making sure he understood his clients' perspectives—their needs and views on their business—before making his recommendations.

3. John realized that he could not rely on most of the network of contacts built during his twenty-five years at Walgreen's. Although the phone rang frequently when he first left Wags, the calls quickly tapered off. As soon as John was no longer boss, mentor, or business giver, his network of associates shrank dramatically. He said that he had to actively solicit business; he couldn't sit back and depend on his reputation and contacts to attract clients.

4. John learned humility. There is nothing more humbling for former executives than being kept waiting for thirty minutes in a prospect's office or having to spell their name three times for a secretary who's never heard of them. Cold calls were especially irksome for John. Irritated by constant interruptions as he tried to talk to a client, John would flash back to the time when the situation was reversed: "I could empathize with how salespeople felt when they called on me," he said. "I'm sure they thought I wasn't paying attention to them."

Before Becoming a Consultant

Now that you've read about one consultant, let's combine his story with others and glean some useful information about this entrepreneurial endeavor.

What type of executive makes the best or most successful consultant? According to what I've learned, the factors discussed in this section of the chapter are the ones that will increase your chances of success.

Match Your Consultancy With Your Corporate Area of Expertise

Stick to what you know. It's unlikely that an MIS executive will try to become a marketing consultant. However, the MIS executive might be tempted to specialize in a trendy new system, seeing a large market there, rather than the system with which he or she is more familiar. It's far better to focus on your area of expertise initially and expand into other areas only after your business is solidly established. Revenue must lead expansion, not follow it. At first, survival is paramount.

Make a Commitment to Consulting

I've talked to other executives besides John Seastone who were initially reluctant to make a total commitment—they became de facto consultants, being drawn into the field rather than jumping in with both feet. Unlike other entrepreneurial fields, consulting doesn't require a significant investment in equipment, people, or office space. But it does require an emotional and intellectual commitment. Consultants who are successful generally throw themselves into their work—they spend their waking hours coming up with new ways of marketing themselves and dream about effective strategies they can suggest to clients. More than any other type of entrepreneur, a consultant's fate is tied to his or her determination and energy.

Don't Rely on Your Corporate Contacts

As John Seastone learned, you can expect only limited help from contacts you established at the corporation. Even if you start out with your former corporation as a client, don't expect the relationship to last forever. Similarly, you'll find that many of those who promised you business when you became a consultant won't fulfill their promises. They were loyal to the corporation, not to a specific corporate executive (meaning you). More than one consultant has found the cupboard bare when he or she neglected to build a network of noncorporate contacts.

Become More Reflective and Analytical and Less Judgmental

You can't treat clients like vendors or employees. If you try to dictate solutions to them—even if they're the right solutions—

you'll get yourself in trouble. Although you may have had a tendency to give orders as a manager, you can't do this with people who hire you. Learn to tailor reports—oral and written—to your clients, taking into consideration each client's personality, needs, objectives, etc.

Capitalize on Your Complementary Expertise

Your clients will pride themselves on how well they know their business. Don't presume you know more about the nuts and bolts of their company than they do. Because you worked at a large corporation, you may think and act like a big fish in a small pond, but behave that way with your clients and they'll throw you out of the pond. Instead, focus on the areas where they lack knowledge you possess. They might know manufacturing backward and forward but be weak in marketing or financial controls; therefore, position yourself as an expert in their areas of weakness.

Market Yourself With a Vengeance

One of the most difficult tasks for executive-consultants is selling themselves. Many of them find it undignified; they aren't used to cold calling and rude secretaries. If you're going to make it as a consultant, though, you'll have to overcome your aversion to self-promotion. Use all the marketing tools at your disposal—public relations, advertising, direct mail, brochures. You'll also have to work phones and rooms, constantly adding to your network. It's an ongoing process; you can never have too many contacts, prospects, and clients. Prepare yourself for rejection and small failures—they are inevitable byproducts of aggressive marketing. Take hope from the fact that you're selling something of value, that you possess hard-earned knowledge gained at a top corporation that will be useful to clients who need what you know.

Positives and Negatives

Certain aspects of consulting engender strong positive and negative responses among former executives. I've created a checklist of the most common pros and cons (Figure 8-1). Examine it closely for factors that apply to you. If you find that the pluses outweigh the minuses, consulting makes sense.

Executives Who Make the Best Consultants

Although I don't believe anyone can predict with 100 percent accuracy whether a given executive will succeed or fail as a consultant, I've found that it *is* possible to make reasonably educated guesses based on certain criteria. I've translated these criteria into the following questions:

▶ Are you between ages 35 and 55 with at least ten years of corporate experience behind you?
▶ Is your area of consultancy directly in line with your area of expertise as a corporate executive?
▶ Do you have a significant amount of marketing/selling experience with the corporation?

Figure 8-1. The consultant's checklist.

Positives	Negatives
Small financial investment	Isolation
Flexible work schedule	Constant selling
Diversity of assignments	Difficult clients
No employees (at least at the start-up stage)	Lack of resources
	Lack of structure
Ability to work independently	Feeling of being an "outsider"
Use of knowledge acquired at the corporation	Financial limitations imposed by selling a finite commodity—the consultant's time

- ▸ Were you a middle manager or above?
- ▸ Did you develop a network of contacts within and outside of the corporation with relative ease?
- ▸ Did you enjoy corporate assignments that were challenging and diverse (as opposed to enjoying assignments that required little homework and few new approaches)?
- ▸ Are you going into consulting with the idea that you'll do it until you retire (as opposed to taking consulting assignments as a stopgap measure until you find something better in the corporate world)?
- ▸ Did you dislike delegating tasks and relying on others?
- ▸ Were you curious about how the ideas you came up with at the corporation would work for other companies in different situations?
- ▸ Did you like the brainstorming aspect of your corporate job and dislike the detail work involved in implementation?

Even if you answered yes to all the preceding questions, you may still fail as a consultant for a variety of "external" reasons—lack of funds or revenue, inadequate demand for your consulting skill, too much competition. In other words, there's risk, and every entrepreneur, consultant or not, runs it. But if you answered yes to all the questions, or to the majority of them, and you want to become an entrepreneur, consulting is a logical choice.

Keep in mind that there are many types of consultants. *Consulting*, in fact, is an umbrella term for a wide variety of endeavors. You can be a data-processing consultant, a marketing consultant, a management consultant. Your consultancy can specialize in a narrow area or be more generalized. Although most consultants start out as lone operators, some consulting businesses employ hundreds of other consultants. You can consult locally, regionally, or nationally.

No matter what type of consultant you become, however, your success will ride on one key factor: knowledge. To the extent that you have or obtain knowledge that others lack, and to the extent that a market is in need of that knowledge, your consulting venture will do well. For instance, I know of a few

MIS executives who worked for a corporation that invested heavily in new IBM technology. These executives learned the technology—how to set it up and use it—better than anyone else. When they saw the technology take off—corporations throughout the country were demanding it—the executives left their corporation and established a consulting business, advising companies about how to buy, set up, customize, and support IBM's new technology. Needless to say, this consulting business was phenomenally successful.

Before becoming a consultant, audit your knowledge base. Ask yourself:

- What do I know better than anyone else?
- Are there companies out there that could benefit from what I know?
- Can I expand my knowledge quickly and easily to make my expertise even more marketable?

Corporate managers with significant experience usually can answer these questions affirmatively. At the very least, they're more likely to give affirmative answers than nonexecutive-entrepreneurs. Perhaps that's why so many former executives become successful consultants.

Chapter 9

Retailing

When you're merely thinking about your entrepreneurial choices, retailing is the easiest one to romanticize. You can see yourself happily running an elegant restuarant, a trendy boutique, or a store filled with precious antiques. Retailing seems as far removed from the daily grind of corporate life as you can possibly imagine.

To a certain extent, all this is true. But as with any business, retailing has its mundane routines, its ulcer-causing problems. Obviously, the problems and opportunies are as varied as the types of retailing businesses. There are big differences between running a supermarket, a chili parlor, a sporting-goods store, and a car-repair shop. Because it would be impossible to discuss the peculiarities of every type of retailing venture, my observations will focus on the characteristics that all retailing establishments have in common.

To give you a sense of what it's like for a corporate executive to make the transition to an entrepreneurial retail business, I'll relate the story of John Hall, the owner of Goose Island Brewery, one of Chicago's hottest new restaurants.

From Boxes to Breweries

After receiving his MBA, John Hall joined Container Corporation and stayed for the next twenty-one years. During his tenure, John rose steadily through the ranks, beginning as a plant controller, working his way through the financial department, transferring laterally into planning, becoming vice-president of planning for the company and then vice-president and operations manager for the shipping-container business.

When John first joined Container, the company was acquired by Montgomery Ward. It was a tumultuous time as the employees adjusted to new ownership. When Mobil Corporation acquired the company years later, John was worried. He had already witnessed the upheaval caused by an acquisition and wasn't looking forward to seeing history repeat itself. Still, he stayed. Then, rumors began circulating that Mobil was going to sell Container. Said John:

> There was no way I was going to go through that again. Mobil is a fine corporation, and they did many good things for Container. But I was in my mid-forties, and I just didn't want to deal with the changes, with people setting policy in New York or some other place without your input.

John started to explore his entrepreneurial options. He and a few associates considered buying a company, but the deal never worked out. John, however, was in an entrepreneurial frame of mind. During a plane flight, he picked up an airline magazine and was fascinated by an article about microbreweries. At about the same time, in July 1986, when Mobil sold Container, John's boss told him that there was going to be a lot of new assignments and wondered what John would be interested in. "I'm interested in getting the best deal possible and getting out of here," John bluntly replied. Looking back, John said, he felt that if he hadn't left then, he would never have left—that that was the time to strike out on his own.

As John was going through outplacement, the microbrewery article stuck in his mind. He learned a great deal about the business by finding some consultants who were ex-brewers and convincing them to let him pick their brains and by visiting different breweries.

The next step was raising money to start his own microbrewery. By enlisting the help of friends and business associates, he gathered substantial funds. The remainder was obtained through a bank loan. John was surprised that his local bank—as opposed to a "downtown" bank—was willing to lend him the money. He had assumed that the banking connections he had made as a container-corporation executive would be required to facilitate a quick and easy loan.

John was convinced his microbrewery was viable. He had done his research. One statistic stood out in his mind: Import beers had been growing at an annual rate of 15 percent for ten years while the overall beer market was flat. That statistic fit a larger societal trend—people were becoming more interested in satisfying their personal tastes via quality products.

Then, reality hit home. The more research John conducted, the more obvious it became that to make the microbrewery successful, he'd need a long time line. He learned that he'd have to enter the promotional wars, fighting other breweries with far more resources to get his beer on the shelves and in taverns and restaurants. "Unfortunately, I was forty-five years old. I had a family and a hefty mortgage to support," he said. "If I was going to get into something, it would have to give me a good, relatively quick return on my investment."

That's when the idea of a combination microbrewery-restaurant came to him. John realized that he could make more money selling beer at a higher price by the glass than selling it at a lower price by the keg and that he could attract more customers by selling food along with the beer.

Although John had no restaurant experience, he quickly found people who did. In 1987, he recruited a manager from the TGI Fridays chain; shortly thereafter, he found a brewmaster. John also contacted a friend of his who worked at the Board of Trade and was involved in another restaurant. His friend wasn't interested in a second restaurant investment but *was* interested in a joint real estate venture. Since John had learned how crucial location was to a restaurant's success, he brought his friend in as a partner. Together they scouted different buildings throughout Chicago. They were looking for a big, old building with adequate parking and sufficiently isolated from surrounding dwellings so that the noise from the restaurant-bar wouldn't provoke complaints.

They finally found the perfect location in the Clyborn corridor, a former industrial strip near affluent Lincoln Park that was just beginning to be rejuvenated. Goose Island Brewery opened in 1988 and has been a tremendous success, drawing standing-room-only crowds and praise from critics.

Valuable Corporate Lessons

Restaurants are a risky type of venture. They're especially risky for people new to the business, like John Hall. But he had an advantage over other restaurant entrepreneurs: His years in the financial department at Container, as well as his operations and planning background, made it unlikely that he'd commit a financial blunder. John understood how to create a budget; he knew the importance of contingency planning, of not building too tight a budget. He understood the bidding and rebidding process with suppliers. "Despite my experience, we still ended up exceeding our budget," he remarked. "But we didn't exceed it by a fatal amount."

The second important resource John brought from his corporate years was contacts. Not only did his business associates provide financial support for his restaurant, but many of the people he knew became customers, helping spread the word about Goose Island. In addition, he had Container Corporation create his menus, eye-catching folders of brown corrugated paper.

Third, John found a number of similarities between running his corporate department and running the restaurant-brewery. "At Container, I had to make decisions that influenced the bottom line as well as supervise people. In many ways, I'm doing the same thing here, just on a smaller scale."

John's planning expertise was especially relevant to his business. He understood how to research a market, how to incorporate that research into a plan with financial objectives, and how to implement the plan and monitor the results. This planning acumen enabled John to run and expand his business at a reasonable pace, avoiding the pitfalls of overexpansion that doom many restaurant operations whose owners are decieved by their initial success.

Container vs. Goose Island: Likes and Dislikes

John Hall readily admits that he wishes he'd made his entrepreneurial move earlier. Although he enjoyed his years with Container, he loves his restaurant-brewery and takes an intense personal pride in the business's success. When he describes his brewing process or invites visitors to taste a new menu item his chef has just made, he talks with far more enthusiasm than he does about his accomplishments at Container. He says that if he had known then what he knows now, he would have opened the restaurant ten years ago. He might not have accumulated all the resources that have served him well, but says he would have been much further along today.

"One of the things I like best about this business is the security," he maintains. "I'm talking about security from the standpoint that at the corporation, somebody else had control over what I was going to do tomorrow or where I was going to live. Here, *I* have control."

John also enjoys the "action" of the restaurant business. He was in staff positions much of his time at Container, removed from the firing line. Running Goose Island, he's intimately involved in all the details: He's constantly talking to customers, making decisions about supplies, promoting the restaurant. He maintains that it's a great business for someone who loves wrapping himself up in an enterprise and having a profound influence over how it does.

Asked to name the most difficult aspect of being a restaurant entrepreneur, he talks about adjusting to a noncorporate culture:

> There's a business mentality in most large corporations, where people operate from a base of knowledge and experience. As a manager, you can assume your people have a shared set of skills and a way of conducting themselves. In the restaurant, that's not always the case. People won't automatically do things the way you want or expect. You need to impose discipline, get involved with all the details. For instance, at the corporation, rules were sometimes bent without harm. Here, if somebody bends a rule, it sets a bad precedent. If one person gets away with something, everyone gets the message that this behavior is acceptable. And it's not.

Another negative is the time commitment. "You can't take a break," John says. "At least, you can't take one the way you could at the corporation. The restaurant business is all-consuming; it demands huge amounts of your time."

When asked whether he misses corporate life, John replies that he misses the people—more specifically, he observes that he misses his peers, people doing the same thing he was doing, comparing notes with them, working toward corporate objectives. "But I don't miss the perks, the trappings of corporate life," he adds. "I had all of that for twenty-one years, and I was ready to move on to something else."

Before Becoming a Retailer

No matter what type of retail establishment you want to start, you can do certain things to improve your odds of success. If you're able to take the following steps, you're moving in the right direction.

Tap Into Your Corporate Resources for Usable Knowledge

John Hall had assembled an almost ideal collection of skills and contacts for his restaurant-brewery venture. Although he didn't do so with that goal in mind, it worked out that way.

Assess your resources and determine how they match the needs of your retail business. Identify not only the resources you possess but the ones you lack. If, for instance, you're going to start an exclusive men's clothing store and you lack selling experience, find someone with that experience whom you can either learn from or hire.

Create a Worst-Case-Scenario Budget and Gather the Necessary Funds

Executives who go into retailing chronically underestimate their capital requirements. This field is volatile, and you should plan for unexpected expenses. If you don't have the financial expertise to create the kind of budget that such a venture requires, find someone who can help you.

In addition, make sure you have explored every funding alternative to gather as much seed money as possible (see Chapter 13, "Funding"). A store is like an old house: There's always something that needs fixing or improving. On the plus side, you'll find that your friends and associates might be more willing to invest in a retail venture than another type of entrepreneurial enterprise. Businesses like restaurants, bars, and boutiques are "fun" investments; people are attracted to the theatrical aspect of retailing and enjoy participating in it. Therefore, look beyond banks and venture-capital groups when trying to secure funding.

Apply the Research and Planning Skills You Acquired at the Corporation to Do Your Homework

If your former company taught you nothing else, it taught you how to research and plan to meet objectives. Unlike a consultancy or product-sales venture, your retail business is probably divorced from your corporate job. As a result, you have a lot to learn. Gather the information you need systematically. Many of the research and planning techniques you mastered at the corporation—surveys, interviewing, market studies—are equally applicable in an entrepreneurial context.

Give Yourself a Competitive Edge

Most retailers operate in a cutthroat competitive environment. It's a different sort of competition than you faced in the corporation. Here, one mistake—such as a poorly chosen location—can destroy the business. Successful retailers like John Hall give themselves as much of an advantage as possible. They avoid major mistakes—a bad location, a sloppily planned budget, underestimating market competitors. Study other successful retailers whose ventures are similar to yours and learn what made them successful. Then, apply those lessons to your own business.

Find Your Niche

If you came from a company that was a market leader or
market challenger, niche marketing might seem like a foreign
concept. But it's a necessary concept for virtually every retailer
who starts fresh. John Hall's niche was a restaurant combined
with a brewery. Your niche could be anything from a shoe store
that caters to people with big feet to a furniture store that
specializes in French imports.

A niche differentiates your retail establishment from others; it gives people a reason to visit your place of business.
Ideally, you'll find a niche with relatively few competitors, at
least in your geographic area.

Positives and Negatives

How do you truly feel about retailing? Have you been seduced
by its surface charms, or do you have a real love for the
business? Certainly, the best way to answer those questions is
through experience, but that can be costly. Executives who
have gone into retailing usually respond in positive and negative ways to certain aspects of their business. Consider the
retailer's checklist (Figure 9-1) and see whether your pluses
outweigh your minuses.

Executives Who Make the Best Retailers

Do you have what it takes to make it as a retailer? To a certain
extent, the answer depends on your attitudes and experiences
as an executive. To see whether you're a merchant at heart,
answer the following questions:

- At the corporation, did you develop a diverse group of
  skills (as opposed to a highly specialized skill set)?
- Did you have much direct contact with your company's
  customers? If so, did you enjoy that contact?

Figure 9-1. The retailer's checklist.

Positives	Negatives
People-oriented business	Long hours
Nonoffice environment	Difficulty dealing with employees (especially those without a business mentality or a college education)
Opportunity to capitalize on a wide range of corporate skills	
Possibility of a significant return on your investment	Substantial financial investment
Interaction with customers	Intense competition
Ability to put your personal stamp on the business	Difficulty finding and working with quality suppliers
	Being at the mercy of economic and other trends

- During your corporate tenure, did you hold any sales or marketing positions?
- Were you mostly in line positions (as opposed to staff positions)? If so, did you prefer line to staff?
- Do you feel that you can count on a number of your corporate contacts for financial and informational assistance when you open your retail business?
- Were you involved in creating and monitoring budgets?
- Are you good with details (as opposed to preferring to delegate detail work to subordinates)?
- Is your family supportive of your desire to undertake a retail venture, and will they tolerate the hours the business will require of you?
- Were you indifferent to the perks, travel, and prestige of working for a major corporation? Or if you weren't entirely indifferent to these trappings, did you at least not attach a high value to them?
- Are you looking forward to the chance to create a retail business that reflects your values and personality?

If you answered yes to the majority of the preceding questions, you probably have the right blend of attitude and experience for a retailing entrepreneurship.

Many of you will choose a retailing business based on something that you enjoy or something that's trendy—you love antiques so you open an antiques store, or you see that frozen yogurt is "in" and you open a frozen-yogurt shop. There's nothing inherently wrong in this except for the following:

- Just because you love what you sell doesn't mean others will follow suit.
- Trends in retailing come and go like changes in the weather.

Therefore, do as much research as possible before embarking on your venture. Some grass-roots investigation will tell you whether there's a significant market in a given area for what you plan to sell. Talk to other established antiques store owners, for instance, and figure out what they've done to be successful. Although trends are more difficult to research, you've probably learned a good lesson from your corporate years: It's far better to jump on a trend at its inception rather than after it has picked up steam. As evidence, count the number of video and computer stores that went under because they failed to catch the first wave of their respective trends.

When thinking about your answers to the questions at the start of this section, concentrate on the one about customers. Retailers must fight for their customers. No other type of venture involves such a fierce battle for customer loyalty. A consultant, for instance, has clients rather than customers— his or her clients are a relatively small, select group, and a consultant usually develops an ongoing relationship with them. Someone involved in product sales has an indirect relationship with customers—the stores serve as an intermediary, a buffer of sorts.

Successful retailers I've worked with have a familiar refrain about their customers: "You've got to listen to what they say and give them what they want." That can translate into numerous things: the right types of products; faster, more courteous service; the proper selection; a money-back policy on returns; convenient store hours and location.

As a corporate executive, you weren't at the mercy of your customers—at least, not directly. As a retailer, you are. The old saying "The customer is always right" applies. Ask yourself the following customer-related questions:

> ▸ Will I enjoy dealing with a large, heterogeneous group of people, each of whom will demand different things of me and my store?
> ▸ Am I skilled at "reading" customers—anticipating what they want and doing everything possible to satisfy their needs?
> ▸ As a former executive, someone who was thought of as the customer by various vendors and suppliers, how will I feel about switching roles? Will I find my new role demeaning—see myself cast as the server rather than the served?
> ▸ Would I be better off creating a store that attracts a particular type of customer—a select group who are more knowledgeable about the products I plan to sell?
> ▸ After creating a mental image of the type of person I think will be my store's customer and then comparing and contrasting that image with the people with whom I worked at the corporation, which of the two do I prefer?

In the corporate world, there is much talk of customer-driven companies. In the entrepreneurial retailer's world, it's more than talk; it's a reality to which former executives must adapt if they are to succeed.

Chapter 10

Product Sales

Many corporate managers understand how to market products. With a superior education in brand management, they're well-versed in the intricacies of bringing products from the idea stage to the stores. Over the years, they've accumulated an impressive amount of knowledge about research and development, manufacturing, advertising, direct marketing, promotion, distribution, and market research.

If this portrait describes you, you may be inclined to become involved in product sales as an entrepreneur. The business opportunities are numerous, from setting up an import venture to becoming a manufacturer's rep to licensing a product from another company. You might even handle all aspects of bringing a product to market—product design, manufacturing, distribution, marketing, etc. (This option, however, usually requires more financial resources than most executive-entrepreneurs have at their disposal.)

Whatever your decision, you will find that selling a product as an entrepreneur is significantly different than marketing a product through a corporation. Not only are you working on a much smaller scale, but you're targeting a much different market. To understand the differences, let's see how one executive fared when he made the transition.

From Electronics Executive to Product-Sales Entrepreneur

Harold Stevenson was a sales executive with a large consumer electronics company in California for fourteen years. In that capacity, he supervised a sales force that sold both products manufactured by his company and those imported from Japan. He'd successfully worked his way up through the company's ranks, gaining experience as a product manager, an ad director, and a salesperson. Each year, Harold would travel to Japan and meet with the company's suppliers. On his last trip, one of the supplier's representatives mentioned that his company had developed a lightweight, portable compact-disk player and claimed it was smaller and weighed less than anything on the market.

Harold was excited about the new product. Upon his return to California, he prepared a presentation to his supervisors, hoping to persuade them to take on the product. They refused. Although they agreed that the product had potential, they felt that it was a bit removed from their product line and would be difficult to sell. Furthermore, because the company had experienced three bad quarters in a row, they weren't willing to make the financial commitment the new product would require.

Harold was upset. He was convinced the lightweight CD player was marketable and felt the company's refusal was shortsighted. In fact, this wasn't the first time that Harold had run into problems with management. In the past few years, the company had changed, or so Harold thought. For the first decade of his employment, the organization had been an exciting place to work, growing quickly and encouraging employee innovation. Recently, however, it had become much more conservative in its outlook; a new CEO seemed overly concerned with quarterly performance as opposed to long-term growth.

Harold had considered leaving twice in recent years. On the first occasion, he had an offer from a competitor. On the second, some friends had asked him to join them in a start-up software company. Harold had declined the latter offer because he wasn't really interested in the software business. But he was intrigued by the basic idea—the idea of being on his own.

This time, though, he was ready. First, he created a business plan for a new company that would sell the lightweight CD player. Then, he showed the plan to a group of investors he knew; they agreed to finance the venture in return for 40 percent equity in the business. Using his many corporate contacts, Harold signed up a sales-broker group to sell the product

into consumer electronics outlets, contacted an advertising
agency that his former employer had fired two years ago
(unjustly, Harold thought), and got a great deal on office space
from a friend who had room in his building. After finding a
warehouse to store his inventory and signing an agreement
with the Japanese supplier, Harold formally tendered his resignation.

Almost immediately, Harold ran into problems, including
a significant number of defective products in the first ship-
ment, difficulty obtaining distribution in key stores, and an
advertising campaign that was very creative and image-ori-
ented but failed to generate many sales.

Harold found himself working around the clock—spending
vast amounts of time traveling to Japan to iron out the problems with the supplier, visiting the ad agency to come up with
a new campaign, and accompanying his sales-broker team as
they called on store reps. Despite Harold's valiant attempts to
remedy the problems, he was making very little headway.

Looking back, Harold said that he was introducing his new
product just as he would have done at the corporation:

> That was my mistake. I failed to understand that I
> couldn't force distribution; that an ad campaign has
> to be sales-oriented, not image-oriented; that it's very
> difficult for a one-man operation to deal effectively
> with an overseas supplier. From a business-textbook
> standpoint, I was doing everything right. From an
> entrepreneurial perspective, I was doing everything
> wrong.

Harold is now in the process of trying to salvage what's
left of his business by selling his lightweight CD player through
catalogs that market state-of-the-art high-tech electronics.
He's slashed his overhead and projects that the business will
make its first profit in the next quarter.

Valuable Corporate Lessons

Despite the problems Harold encountered, he was an excellent
candidate for a product-sales entrepreneurship.

First, he possessed a talent for spotting salable products—a talent honed over many years with the corporation. As Harold observed, "I've been trained to identify a product's strengths and weaknesses and how to capitalize on those strengths in the sell-in sell-through process." And very obviously, Harold's corporate contacts enabled him to strike a deal with the Japanese company for the portable CD player. Those contacts also enabled him to assemble a team to bring the product to market.

Finally, his corporate experience provided Harold with an understanding of the available options that proved invaluable when his first effort failed. He'd been exposed to catalog marketing and recognized it as a viable alternative. Not only did Harold recognize the alternative, but he had enough knowledge about the direct-marketing process to proceed quickly.

Consumer Electronics Company vs. Product-Sales Venture: Likes and Dislikes

Harold is still enthusiastic about being an entrepreneur, despite his initial mistakes: "As a sales manager at the corporation, I always thought of the line of products I was responsible for as 'my' products. But they really weren't; they were the corporations. Now, the CD player, for better or worse, really is my product. Psychologically, that's a great feeling."

Harold, like many of the other executive-entrepreneurs I've talked to, also relishes his independence from corporate bureaucracies and red-tape-bound decision making. He says that this independence speeds up the selling process, that there's a much shorter wait to see the results of one's labors:

> Sometimes at my former employer, it would take a year or even longer from product conception to implementation to sales results. By the time you learned the results, you were already somewhat distanced from the product; you'd be involved in some other project. Now, everything moves much faster, and that's gratifying for someone like me who hates to wait.

On the negative side, Harold misses the large corporate sales-support staff. When he started his business, Harold says he was anxious to do everything he could to gain distribution and sales for the CD player as quickly as possible. Unfortunately, he couldn't devote all of his time to that objective. There were so many tangential details to deal with—finding an office, an ad agency, a warehouse, a lawyer for contracts— that he was unable to focus all his efforts on his primary goal. He offers the following thoughts on how this affected the success of his venture:

> It was frustrating. I wish I could have assigned some of those tasks to other people, as I did at my former job. I think if I had had more time for research and thinking, I might not have made the mistakes that I did. If I were to do it again, I think I'd try to gather more seed money so that I could hire an assistant to handle the detail work.

Before Starting a Product-Sales Business

The tale of Harold Stevenson should serve as a caution to other executive-entrepreneurs. Based on Harold's experiences as well as those of other product-sales people I've talked to, I'd advise you to take the following steps before opening your business.

Imagine Selling Your Corporation's Products as an Entrepreneur

This first exercise is easy and enjoyable and will yield a number of valuable insights. Take a product that you know fairly well and map its history—the research and development, test-marketing, distribution, and promotional strategy that introduced it to the market. Then, create a parallel "history," only this time create it as if you were introducing the product on your own. You don't have to do any research. Use your instincts and common sense to develop a realistic plan. Give yourself a feasible budget, think about the contacts you might tap, figure out the resources you'll need.

Finally, compare and contrast the two plans. The differences will be instructive. You'll probably find that obstacles your company easily overcame will be much harder for you to hurdle as an independent businessperson. Conversely, you may find that you can move more quickly and be more flexible in your entrepreneurial product introduction. With this knowledge, you'll be better-prepared to sell a product without the benefit of corporate resources.

Think About What Type of Product You Enjoy Selling and Are Qualified to Sell

The right product for one entrepreneur is the wrong product for another. If you've worked with consumer food products all your corporate life, you may not have sufficient experience to sell office supplies. On the other hand, if you've sold widgets for your entire corporate career and can't stand the thought of selling another one, you might want to find a different product (although perhaps it would be wise to choose one that targets the market with which you're familiar).

One entrepreneur told me of an exercise she used that might also help you. Create a list of product categories that you've worked in—hardware, computers, etc. Then winnow that list down by placing a check mark next to the categories that excite you—ones whose existing products interest you and whose prospects for expansion seem bright (i.e., you feel there would be a good potential market for new products.) Once you've arrived at a few, select categories, create a list of products in each category. Look over the lists and check off two or three products that seem to stand out. Trust your instincts. If a product makes your pulse race, that may be the one that will launch your second career.

Of course, you'll still have to extensively research the product and market you chose. But at least you've picked something that makes sense, given your personal preferences and experience.

Make a List of Resources

More so than the entrepreneurial consultant or retailer, you're going to need help in product sales. Harold Stevenson, for instance, wisely lined up a number of resources—an ad agency, a foreign manufacturer, a sales-broker group—from his corporate past. As a seller of products, you're dependent on many other people besides yourself. Unless you have the money to set up a turnkey operation, you'll require assistance with everything from sales to advertising to manufacturing to public relations. Theoretically, though, you're in a better position than a nonexecutive-entrepreneur when it comes to seeking help. Either you've worked with the people you'll need, or you have contacts who can refer you to the right sources.

Before starting your business, make a list of all the products or services you'll require, together with the individuals and companies who can deliver them. If you come up with a blank for some of the necessary resources—you don't know any ad-agency executives, for instance—think about who might serve as good referral sources. Perhaps you've worked with a brand manager at your former company who used to be an agency account executive.

If possible, contact the resources on your list before you leave your organization. You have more clout with many of these people as an executive than as an entrepreneur. Tell them what you plan to do and see how or whether they can help you. This is time-consuming work, and it's better to get as much of it as possible out of the way before you're on your own.

Positives and Negatives

Product sales as an independent businessperson involves a number of advantages and disadvantages. If you can capitalize on the former and avoid the latter, you will greatly enhance your odds for success. The product-sales checklist shown in Figure 10-1 should help you in this regard, as will the following subsections, which discuss each of the positives and negatives in detail.

Ability to Use Alternative Selling Vehicles

As an ex-executive, you'll probably be inclined to sell your product in a manner similar to the way products were sold by

Figure 10-1. The product-sales checklist.

Positives	Negatives
Ability to use alternative selling vehicles	Distribution walls
Target-market options	Knockoffs
Ways to focus on unique product benefits	Failing to shift product gears
Opportunities to test and retest	
Profitable pricing	

your former employer. After all, it's the sales method you know best, and it may be appropriate. Then again, it may be inappropriate because of the type of product you're offering or because of your size, prospective customers, or financial resources. I've found that many entrepreneurs involved in product sales successfully capitalize on alternative selling vehicles. Consider the following list.

- ► Catalogs
- ► Direct mail
- ► Telemarketing
- ► Limited retail distribution in a certain type of store (discount, boutique, etc.)
- ► Via a second party (through a larger company, a premium house, an exporter, etc.)
- ► Public relations

The primary advantage of these alternative vehicles is cost savings. Direct mail, for instance, doesn't require a sales force and the other attendant costs of retail distribution. Although you might not be familiar with these approaches from your corporate years, each can be studied by reviewing the available literature or hiring a consultant.

Some of you might regard these alternatives as too pedestrian. If your dream is to see your product in national distribution in all the leading stores, it could be difficult to accept a catalog approach. On the other hand, you might regard these alternatives as stepping-stones toward your dream. More than one nationally distributed product began as a catalog or direct-mail item. If it succeeds in a catalog, you have a track record that will attract attention and impress retailers and investors.

If yours is a business-to-business product, the same advice holds true. Let's say your product is an imported personal computer. It's going to be tough for you to compete with the sales reps from established manufacturers—you don't have the name, the sales force, the promotional materials, or the time to compete. But other methods are available to you. You may be able to strike a deal with an established company that sells to your target market but whose products are not competitive with yours. See whether such a company would be willing to take your product on for a percentage. Or perhaps you can concentrate your selling efforts on trade shows and industry conventions, in an attempt to gain a foothold by letting prospective customers try your product in a more neutral setting.

I know of one ex-executive who used public relations as her sole sales vehicle. She'd created a software program that simulated various business situations, allowing users to ascertain their business acumen by testing their responses to these situations. This entrepreneur, drawing upon public relations skills gained in her former corporation's marketing department, wrote news releases announcing the introduction of this software and sent them to general business and selected trade publications. The resulting publicity generated hundreds of leads, many of which she turned into sales. Because her product was so conducive to publicity, she continued to rely on public relations tools during the first two years of her business, earning a six-figure income by the end of that period.

Target-Market Options

Corporations use target marketing, but their targets are big. Many executive-entrepreneurs I've worked with have a hard time setting realistic targets. Their inclination is to shoot wide of the mark. Instead of targeting all males between the ages of 25 and 35 with an income of between $40,000 and $60,000, they fix on males between the ages of 20 and 50 with an income in excess of $30,000. If someone suggests that they narrow their focus, their typical response is, "That's too small a slice of the pie." At the corporation, that response might have been appropriate. But successful product-sales entrepreneurs feast on such small slices.

Sketch a profile of your best customer. Include demographics, psychographics, and life-style. Hone that profile until it seems as if you're describing a single person. Then fine-tune your marketing and merchandising efforts so that you're selling to that individual.

Don't be afraid to start with only one market or one region of the country. Don't feel as if you have to gain distribution in the major stores in a given area. As a novice entrepreneur without a track record, you need to establish yourself. If you aim too high, you're bound to be disappointed. If you try to measure your success against what you achieved at the corporation, you're bound to come up short. Think small, at least in the beginning. Survival is the first step toward success.

Such a strategy is the way entrepreneurs gain footholds in a market. As a general rule, the narrower your target market, the more successful your initial sales efforts will be.

Ways to Focus on Unique Product Benefits

Through advertising, public relations, promotions, direct mail, and one-on-one contact, you'll promote your product. As Harold Stevenson learned the hard way, though, there's a difference between promoting a corporate product and an entrepreneurial product. As an entrepreneur, your promotion should be straightforward and product-oriented. It should answer the "why" questions: Why should a customer buy the product? Why should a chain stock it? All the things you promoted at the corporation—image, attitude, awareness—become secondary. You must convince people that your product is salable and buyable.

It's fine if you can achieve other objectives as well—creating a mystique for your product or suggesting that it fits a certain life-style. But as I've stressed throughout this book, the paramount concern of the beginning entrepreneur is revenue. You need to generate it fast. If you have a product that offers a unique, demonstrable benefit, emphasize that above all else.

Opportunities to Test and Retest

Corporations test-market; entrepreneurs experiment. Test-marketing is an elaborate procedure that requires a considerable investment and well-defined measurement procedures. Experimentation requires tinkering and instinct.

For you to sell your product successfully, you need to find the right approach—the right combination of markets, advertising, personal selling, distribution, etc. The way to find that combination is through experimentation. Although you probably don't have the resources to conduct research on the scale of the corporation, virtually every entrepreneur who has been with a corporation understands the test-marketing process. Try a number of approaches. It might be as simple as designing a few different direct-mail pieces to see which one generates the most replies. Or it might involve some grass-roots research to see what product name gets the best response.

Whatever you do, don't limit yourself to one approach. At the corporation, you had the benefit of numerous experts—e.g., ad agencies, public relations concerns, market-research specialists, sales consultants. Together with your corporate staff, you could come up with the definitive approach. Now, you don't have all that expertise at your disposal. Without it, you may make some mistakes in your product-introduction strategy. Testing gives you the chance to correct those mistakes.

As an entrepreneur, you have to be flexible. You can't lock yourself into strategies and tactics that don't work. Unlike the corporation, you're small enough to adjust quickly to marketplace realities; you don't need approval from a series of higher-ups before making changes. Furthermore, you can test your product without elaborate focus groups and scanner data. It's simply a matter of gauging positive and negative responses to what you're offering and then making the indicated changes.

Profitable Pricing

Executive-entrepreneurs often underprice or overprice their products. Sometimes, they rely on pricing formulas left over from their corporate jobs. Other times, they fall in love with their products and boost the price sky-high, figuring that what they're selling is worth it. Or they become pessimists, keeping the price low because they can't believe that anyone will purchase their merchandise.

It's far better to price a product so that you make a reasonable profit. Do some financial calculations to determine what that reasonable profit is. For instance, if you make a three-dollar profit per unit sold and you estimate that you'll sell one thousand units per month, ask yourself, "Can my business survive on $3,000 per month during its first year?"

The next question to ask yourself is, "How is my product priced compared to competitive products in its category?" If all the other products are priced lower, you had better have an incredibly compelling argument for your higher price. As a rule, executive-entrepreneurs can price their products below those of larger competitors. You probably have far less overhead, giving you the room to come in at a lower price. Remember, it's easier to raise prices than it is to cut them. The former tactic is expected by the marketplace and warranted if the demand is sufficiently high; the latter tactic suggests desperation.

Distribution Walls

Big companies have clout with retailers. Although it's no longer as easy as it once was for them to force distribution, they have enough power to get the majority of their products into the stores they've targeted. You don't. Shelf space has never been tighter, and you can expect to pay hefty slotting allowances if you want to get into a store where space is tight (such as a big supermarket).

Prepare yourself for resistance and don't become discouraged. No matter how great your product may be, you're going to have to work hard to convince a store buyer of that fact. If it's a choice between your homemade cookies and a new line from Keebler, the buyer will probably choose Keebler.

Therefore, set realistic distribution goals. It may be that you'll only be able to get into ma-and-pa stores at first or that you'll have to accept the worst shelf space. If you don't have contacts with the store buyers you're targeting, it's wise to enlist the services of someone who does. Find a sales broker with a track record for securing distribution in your product category. In the distribution business, such contacts are essential.

Knockoffs

You introduce your product, and it sells like hotcakes. The orders are pouring in, a trade magazine profiles you and your venture, the phone is ringing constantly. You've got it made. You've got it made, that is, until another company knocks off your product.

It's inevitable. You may have experienced the same situation at your former organization. Big companies frequently can hold their ground in the face of knockoffs. They have numerous weapons at their disposal—price wars that force the knockoff manufacturer out of business, advertising blitzes that swamp financially strapped competitors. Unless you have significant financial resources, you can't respond to knockoffs the same way. If a big company knocks off your product, the odds are that it can sweep you off the shelves. You are immune to knockoffs only if you have the type of product that can be patented or your product is too difficult for others to copy (e.g., it requires manufacturing technology that your competitors lack.)

Still, you have a chance of surviving. When your product takes off, don't start spending money as if you'll always have the market to yourself. Expect competition, conserve your resources, and dig in for a long battle. Because yours is the original product, you have a natural marketing advantage— you're going to build considerable brand loyalty. If you can stay in the game, you may be able to hold on to your niche.

Another option is to seek help. Hot products attract investors. It might be possible to bring in partners to provide the financial backing you'll need in order to hold on to your market share. Or you may find a larger company willing to buy your product and market it under its own name.

Failing to Shift Product Gears

Corporations hate to admit failure, especially when it comes to new products. Too many careers are on the line for anyone to concede quickly, "We made a mistake." Although there are some exceptions to this rule, most large organizations seem to take forever before they pull a product from distribution. Their tendency is to tinker with the marketing, to try to make an adjustment that will resurrect dormant sales.

You may not have the time or money to make such adjustments. George Hovesepian didn't. A former engineering executive, George was also an inventor. In his spare time, he'd been working on a toy robot that he'd created from scratch. His kids and their friends loved playing with it, and it dawned on him that it might be a marketable toy. After he lost his job when his company was acquired, George contacted a toy-design company. After he demonstrated his robot for them, the staff members were very enthusiastic, and George entered into a partnership with the company. Unfortunately, George's basement-shop design work didn't translate well into the manufacturing process. It proved to be both difficult and costly to produce the robot in quantity. Yet George persevered. He was so wrapped up in his dream of making millions from his toy robot that he stubbornly kept going, hiring manufacturing and design consultants in an attempt to remedy the problem. Even after his partners withdrew from the project, George still believed the situation could be corrected.

George probably would have used up his entire savings if not for a suggestion from one of the consultants he hired. The consultant told George that the robot design might be of interest to one of his chemical-processing clients; the client company was looking for robotic technology to deal with a tricky chemical-handling process at its plant. Reluctantly, George agreed to a meeting with representatives of the company. After a number of meetings, they made a sizable offer for George's robot, which he accepted.

The point of this story is that your vision for your product might not jibe with marketplace realities. If that's the case, don't throw good money after bad. One of the advantages you have as an entrepreneur is the ability to act quickly. You don't have to receive approvals from a chain of command before jettisoning a product. Like George, you may find that your product is salable to a different market than the one you originally targeted. Or in the course of trying to sell your product, you may discover another product that is more marketable.

Whatever the situation, keep your options open. Successful entrepreneurs often have a history of unsuccessful products; many proudly discuss all the failures that preceded their successes. Although such a track record might hurt a corporate manager, it is far less harmful to an entrepreneur. As long as you get out of a deal before it saps your finances and your motivation, you should be fine.

Executives Who Make the Best Product-Sales Entrepreneurs

Do you think you're better-suited to a product-sales business than to a consulting or retailing venture? The following questions should help you make that determination:

- Have you ever been a brand or product manager?
- Did you have a feeling of personal satisfaction when a product you were responsible for did well (earned a high market share, for instance)?
- At the corporation, did you try to understand your products inside and out? Did you want to know everything about them, even if such knowledge wasn't strictly necessary for your job performance? Did you want to learn how the product was made, every point of difference between it and competitive products, etc.?
- Did you develop a broad spectrum of contacts that will serve you well as an independent product salesperson?

- ▸ Have you had much exposure to such marketing disciplines as public relations, sales promotion, advertising, direct marketing, sales, and distribution?
- ▸ Did you ever work on licensing agreements?
- ▸ Do you enjoy orchestrating the efforts of a diverse group of specialists to achieve a common goal?
- ▸ Are you comfortable with and skilled at adjusting your strategy when market conditions and other factors call for quick shifts?
- ▸ At the corporation, did you enjoy working on projects that required target or regional marketing tactics? How about projects that required working with smaller budgets to achieve very specific and limited objectives?

If you answered yes to most of the preceding questions, then you're off to a good start. But there's one catch: Your success in the product-sales category, more so than in consulting and retailing, depends on one overriding factor: the product you choose. If it's a terrible product, nothing else you do will matter. The best salesperson in the world can't sell a flawed product. Even if it's mediocre, you'll be laboring at a great disadvantage.

Therefore, you need to ask yourself, "Am I able to find a better-than-average product?" Not everyone can. If you're like most executives, you were "handed" products at the corporation; you didn't have to go out and search for them. Either you took over an established line, or you worked with a new-product development team.

Obviously, you don't have to be an inventor to start your own product-sales business. But you do have to "invent" many aspects of a product—how it's packaged, promoted, manufactured, positioned, and so on. You'll need a sixth sense not only to identify a product you think you can sell but also to target the market you think will buy it. If such tasks seem beyond your abilities, think twice about product sales. If, however, you're confident that you can master them, start searching for your better mousetrap.

Chapter 11

Special Situations

What if you don't plan on a consulting, retailing, or product-sales entrepreneurship? Or what if your specific circumstances—your corporate background or type of venture—don't fit the typical pattern? If your situation is unique, this chapter is for you.

From my work and discussions with executive-entrepreneurs, I've found that there are four special situations that merit examination—situations in which many former executives find themselves. They are: (1) the franchise opportunity, (2) the hobby-turned-business, (3) the service business, and (4) the unretired syndrome.

The Franchise Opportunity

Franchises appeal to former executives. They offer an enticing combination: an independent business backed by the support of a large organization. For many ex-executives, franchises are a more comfortable entrepreneurial fit than autonomous operations.

Franchising options abound in personnel, restaurants, and retail stores. They also blossom in trendy industries—computers, tanning salons, frozen-yogurt stores, quick-change oil services.

The biggest mistake executive-franchisees make is to view a franchise as being just like any other business. It's not. It has its own set of advantages and disadvantages, especially for former corporate managers. Here's the story of one such manager.

People Are His Business

Chuck Stuertz spent almost thirty years as a human resources manager with Commonwealth Edison, Maremont, and Signode. A corporate raider tried and failed to take over this last company in 1981. One of the consequences of the raid was significant cost cutting for the next four years, with Chuck being among the many people whose positions were eliminated. Chuck went through outplacement and, for the next two years, tried to find another human resources job with a corporation. What he found instead was a diminishing supply of such jobs and many eager young human resources specialists willing to work for half his former salary.

Although Chuck had never considered starting his own business, it now seemed like a logical move. For one thing, the staffing industry was hot. For another thing, he met a downsized marketing executive who was interested in forming a partnership with him, and a temporary-staffing business sounded promising.

After conducting extensive research, Chuck and his partner began looking for financing. Unfortunately, no bank was interested in lending them the start-up funds. They contacted the National Association of Temporary Services and received a list of franchisors that might make financing easier. Intrigued, Chuck and his partner interviewed the franchisors, sorting through the complex financial agreements that called for franchisees to pay different percentages of their gross revenues in exchange for different services.

Finally, they settled on a group called Adia. The night before Chuck and his partner were to sign the papers, his partner pulled out of the deal. Despite his nervousness, Chuck decided to go ahead on his own. He had $100,000 in savings and severance monies that he was willing to risk on the venture.

At first, everything went amazingly smoothly. Within four months, Chuck's business had broken even (usually, the breakeven point comes much later). Chuck found his corporate experience invaluable. Just as he had sold his employers on human resources programs, he was able to sell customers on

his temporary-staffing services. As the business became profitable, Chuck quickly opened two more offices.

Unfortunately, Chuck's corporate experience hadn't prepared him for the financial strain of too much overhead or
what to do when the economy in his field suffered a downturn.
Things got shaky for a while, but Chuck managed to cut costs
and struggle through a tough period. As of this writing, his
franchise operation is in decent shape.

With hindsight, Chuck was glad that he chose the franchise
route. One of the great advantages of a franchise, he main-
tained, is that it allows you to "hit the ground running." He
said that Adia provided him with marketing materials, an
operating system, and a way to finance the business. "Instead
of spending my time developing all these things, I could concentrate my energies on the actual business."

In addition, Chuck noted that a franchisee gains immediate recognition because of the franchisor's name, latching on
to the name equity that the franchise has acquired over the
years. Such recognition can be especially important to former
executives, who are used to working for a company with an
established reputation in the marketplace.

On the negative side, Chuck found that a franchisee's
entrepreneurial freedom is limited. "Sometimes, you don't
want to use the materials the franchisor gives you, or you want
to come up with your own—like creating your own ads. That's
not possible, at least according to my agreement with Adia."

Another drawback Chuck mentioned is the continuing
service fee that franchisees must pay:

> It's rare to get rich in this business, especially because
> you have to pay that fee as long as you're a franchisee.
> Former execs shouldn't become franchisees because
> they want to make instant millions. My goal, and that
> of other franchisees I know, is to sell their franchises
> sometime down the road at a substantial profit.

Finally, Chuck pointed out that your operating alternatives are limited by your agreement with the franchisor. His
agreement called for him to spend all his time on the business,

making it impossible for him to hire somebody else to run his offices or to do it part-time.

Looking back, Chuck was glad he bought his franchise business, although he voiced a complaint common to many executive-entrepreneurs, not just franchisees: "I wouldn't have waited two years before buying my franchise. Not only did I drain my financial resources during that two-year period, but if I had bought this franchise right after I was terminated, I would be two years closer to my goal."

Franchises From the Executive's Perspective

In order to determine whether you'd make a good franchisee, you need to assess how your attitudes and experience fit with the requirements of franchising. Consider the following issues:

▸ *Does the franchise business dovetail with the skills and knowledge you gained as an executive?* Too many executives choose franchises based on what's "hot." They are seduced by the trendiness of a particular franchise, falsely assuming that if nonexecutives have made money at it, it should be a breeze for them. Ask yourself whether you really know what you're getting into.

▸ *Have you compared the franchise to a similar, but independent, business?* Chuck Stuertz did, and he found that as an independent, he would have trouble with financing; he also decided he didn't want to go through the time-consuming start-up phase that an independent business would require. Remember, though, that as an independent, you will theoretically make more money in the long run. Also, your temperament might be such that you will chafe under the limitations imposed by a franchisor.

▸ *Do your franchise's particular philosophy, strategy, and tactics jibe with those of your former corporation?* Many ex-executives I've worked with learn that the franchise's approach to such matters as marketing is diametrically opposed to their former employer's—the franchise believes in comparative advertising, for instance, whereas the corporation found that it didn't work. Although franchisees are one step removed from the franchisor's culture, they are still affected by it. Investigate what that culture will involve before buying into it.

Now, let's look at the issue of choosing a franchise that is appropriate for you in terms of the services received from the franchisor, the franchisor's business savvy, and your particular goals.

Franchises differ from one another in many ways, perhaps the most important of which is the service fee that franchisees pay and what they receive in return. Chuck Stuertz, for instance, found that the fees ranged widely. He also discovered that a lower fee was not necessarily better than a higher one, since the higher fee was accompanied by more services. Therefore, learn exactly what you'll be receiving for your fee. The best way to do this is by talking to other franchisees, whose names the franchisor should be willing to provide. Those services will range from nothing more than a name to put on your stationery to a variety of ads, promotions, operating systems, and financing. Also remember that more isn't always better. You may have your own ideas for the business and want to structure it without restrictions. Or you may be like Chuck Stuertz and want to avail yourself of the franchisor's services so you can start selling as quickly as possible.

You also need to determine whether your prospective franchisor really understands the business that you're interested in. Adia, for example, is well-versed in the staffing industry and uses franchises to further its corporate goals. Other franchisors, however, know relatively little about their business. If you find the latter is the case, beware! You can expect little substantive help—and you may need help, because you're coming from a corporate world, not a franchising one.

Besides evaluating the franchisor's services and business acumen, think about your own goals before signing a franchise agreement. If you have a great deal of money to invest and you're looking for a sure thing, maybe it makes sense to buy a McDonald's franchise. Established, well-run franchises have very high fees, and if you're able to pay them, you receive a franchise without many flaws. If, on the other hand, you're a young former executive without a lot of cash, your greatest asset is time. It might therefore be wise for you to choose a lower-profile franchise that entails more risk and requires less up-front capital. Some former corporate managers I've talked to regard franchises as investments, much like real estate or securities; they see them as a way to meet retirement goals. If this describes you, examine your contract carefully (better yet, have a lawyer examine it). See whether it allows you to sell your franchise at its market value at any time, no strings attached.

The Hobby-Turned-Business

You're a middle manager who loves to sail, a vice-president of operations who is a food fanatic, a CEO who treasures journeys abroad searching for exotic art. You decide to turn such a hobby into a business. Whether you succeed will depend largely on the extent to which you can distance yourself from what you love and instead view and operate it as a business.

A few years back, *The Wall Street Journal* ran an article about executives who turned their hobbies into businesses. One of the more cautionary examples involved an advertising executive who left her agency to set up a pottery studio. Although she had cherished pottery all her life, she grew to hate it when it became her job—she couldn't stand the business-related tasks that the venture involved, such as hiring assistants or meeting her customers' volume demands. Eventually, she shut the business down and hasn't thrown a pot since.

If you're like most entrepreneurs who open a hobby-related business, your hobby has very little to do with your former corporate job. There's nothing inherently wrong with that, except that it puts you at a disadvantage: Unlike other executive-entrepreneurs, you're not capitalizing on those years of corporate experience. Still, what you lack in "hard" knowledge may be offset by your business skills—budgeting, marketing, distribution, etc. The key is to apply those skills objectively.

It's not easy for hobbyists-turned-entrepreneurs. I know of a plant manager for a major chemical-products company who decided to open a bookstore. An avid reader who couldn't conceive of anything more satisfying than being surrounded by books he cherished and selling them to other readers, he proceeded to stock the store with his favorite books, devoting a significant amount of shelf space to mysteries and science fiction. "I quickly learned that my tastes didn't reflect those of the people in my bookstore's neighborhood," he subsequently observed. "No matter how hard I pushed the books I cared about, people kept coming in asking about ones I didn't have."

Luckily, this former plant manager remembered some lessons from his previous job—lessons about the cost of unused inventory, in particular. With the help of a marketing consultant who had worked for his former employer, he redesigned and restocked the store, targeting his neighborhood market. "It was very difficult for me," he said. "For years, I carried around this vision of what my bookstore would be like. It was hard for me to adapt that vision to reality. I mean, this wasn't just another business—it was something I really cared about."

Before turning your hobby into an entrepreneurial venture, subject your idea to the following analysis:

Analysis of Your Hobby's Business Potential

1. *List the skills acquired as a corporate executive that you think you'll be able to use in your venture.* If your list contains five or more skills, you're in a good position.

2. *Ask a savvy friend or consultant to examine your business plan objectively.* What is his or her reaction? The key comment to listen for is: "I don't think there's much of a market for this." Hobbyists-turned-entrepreneurs are often too wrapped up in their pastime to analyze the market correctly.

3. *Imagine what your daily routine will be like when you turn your hobby into a business.* Then list all the tasks you'll be performing. If, for instance, you're thinking of opening a company to be called Whitewater Excursions, your list of tasks might include planning the trips, booking customers, dealing

with canceled reservations, setting prices, hiring guides, maintaining the rafts, acquiring liability insurance, advertising and promoting your excursions, and establishing contacts with travel agents. After you've listed the tasks, write down your dreams for your business—what you envisioned while sitting in your executive office. If the tasks clash with your vision—if they strike you as uninspiring and mundane—reconsider the venture.

4. *Determine how much income you want to derive from your hobby-related business as well as how much you'll need.* By choosing a hobby as the basis for your entrepreneurial venture, you are automatically committing a sin: You're dictating to the market rather than letting the market dictate to you. Unless your choice happens to coincide with market demands, it could be rough sledding financially. Most entrepreneurs must expect a decline in salary relative to their corporate jobs, at least during the first year or two of entrepreneurship, and the decline will probably be steeper in the case of a business based on a hobby. Estimate the probable decrease in your salary. For most people without significant financial reserves, a drop of 50 percent or more is unacceptable.

5. *Conduct an analysis of competitors.* I've found that businesses derived from hobbies tend to cluster around certain activities: restaurants, bars, outdoor sports (fishing, boating, golf), antiques, collectables, bed-and-breakfasts. That being the case, it's likely that others are already doing what you plan to do. The question is, How many of them are doing it in your targeted market? As an ex-executive, you've done competitive analyses before (or you know someone who can do such an analysis for you). Find out whether the market is saturated. If it is, or if there's healthy competition, think about how you can break through the competitive clutter. The key might be a special skill you acquired as an executive: a genius for promotion, an ability to create and implement unique programs, financial acumen that allows you to operate with lower margins than your competitors. Use that special skill to your advantage.

The Service Business

During the past decade, there's been an explosion in the number and variety of service-based companies—everything from home-cleaning businesses to marketing-services organizations to computer-related ventures. More often than not, ex-executives choose service businesses over product-based ones. The decision is logical, since it's easier and less expensive for a small organization to market services rather than products. But if you've never sold a service before—or if you've never sold one without the backing of a large organization—you should be aware of the special problems and opportunities you'll face, as well as how your corporate background will affect your new enterprise.

Problems and Opportunities

Dallen Peterson made an amazingly successful transition from corporate employee to entrepreneur. I came across his story in *Nation's Business* and am summarizing it here because it's a textbook example of how to create an entrepreneurial service business. For many years, Peterson labored as a top executive with Fairmont Foods, a national dairy and snack-foods company. But when the organization decided to move its headquarters from Omaha to Houston, Peterson reassessed corporate life. Not only didn't he want to move, but he had come to dislike the demands of his job and the vulnerability of his position. He decided to make a change.

Using his savings, a loan, and his profit-sharing money, he started a small snack-foods company. Despite his years of experience in the field, he couldn't make a go of it and sold the business at a loss. But he enjoyed his taste of entrepreneurship and wanted to start a new venture. This time, he decided to try a service business. He liked the idea of selling a service, primarily because it required a relatively small capital investment and because it seemed to be the type of business that was doing well. His wife helped him come up with the idea of a cleaning service for working women, and they began it operating out of their home.

Peterson and his wife distributed fliers, bought cleaning equipment, and cleaned their first customers' homes themselves. They made a few early mistakes common to the service field: poor pricing and offering too many services that weren't equally profitable. But they worked out the kinks, and the business took off. Soon, Peterson's company, called Merry Maids, was selling franchises. (Interestingly, Peterson noted that more than half his franchise owners came from the corporate world.) By 1987, there were four hundred Merry Maid franchises employing four thousand people in forty-two states.

Merry Maids, like many other successful service businesses, are ideal for ex-executives. They offer the following advantages:

- *Low start-up costs:* They can be run out of your home (at least initially) and don't demand a costly investment in inventory or equipment.
- *An outgrowth of consulting:* Many service businesses begin as consulting operations. As a consultant, you can get your feet wet and establish contacts. A number of former executives I've talked to say that they found the transition from offering advice to offering an actual service relatively painless.
- *An idea-driven business:* The best service businesses blossom from the best ideas. Corporations are great teachers of idea generation and implementation. You've had practice in brainstorming new ideas, developing them, creating models for their execution, budgeting for them, and implementing them. The right idea at the right time can take you a long way in the service business.

At the same time, ex-executives make a number of predictable mistakes in this arena. Perhaps the most common one is offering too many services too soon. Your tendency will be to think big—the way your former company taught you to think. Instead of providing one or two critical services, you'll offer five or six. In many instances, the additional four will create more problems than they're worth. For every service, you'll have to establish systems for operating, pricing, and marketing. If those four additional services aren't as profitable as your major ones, they'll drain your time, resources, and capital. The best advice I can give you is, Think small—at least, in the short term.

Another problem is pricing. If you come from a product background, you're used to fixing a price based on product-sales cost and a given industry markup. But how do you price a unique service? How do you price something if you have no competitors whose prices might serve as a standard? It's difficult, and I have no pricing panacea. I can tell you that you'll probably price your service according to the type of company you came from. If your former employer offered premium-priced goods, you'll probably err on the high side. If you worked for a discounter, you may well price your service too low. A logical beginning is to determine the profit margin you want and set the price accordingly.

A third problem is supporting a service business as it expands. Think about an ad agency that goes from one employee to ten, a software-development organization that grows from three to fifteen people, a VCR-repair company that quadruples its size in less than a year. At your former organization, most of you never ran a department that expanded so quickly. It's a shock, but one you should be prepared for. More than any other type of business, service-based ventures must respond immediately to customer demand. Unlike someone who sells products, you can't simply call up a supplier and reorder. Your stock-in-trade is people, and you may have to hire a bunch of them immediately. If you don't have a human resources background, you will probably find yourself making hiring mistakes. An outside search firm or consultant can help you find employees, but at a considerable cost.

What Do You Bring to Your Service Venture?

Although it's very hard to predict how any executive will do as a service-based entrepreneur (primarily because so much depends on the marketability of a given service), a look at your corporate résumé will give you an indication of how well-prepared you are for this type of enterprise. Glance over the following list of skills and experience that will serve as assets in opening a service business. If your corporate background includes a majority of these assets, a service business may pay off for you.

Service-Business Assets

- ▸ My former company sold services rather than products.
- ▸ My company sold products, but I was involved in the customer-service end of the business.
- ▸ I had a reputation as an "idea person."
- ▸ I gained significant experience in pricing products or services.
- ▸ I was involved in at least one start-up program, taking it from the idea stage through research and development to implementation.
- ▸ I did a significant amount of hiring or worked in my company's human resources department.
- ▸ I have a good grounding in cash-flow principles. (As service businesses expand, cash-flow expertise becomes critical. On-time payment is a thorny problem for virtually any service business.)

The Unretired Syndrome

Maybe, when your company cuts costs, you grabbed its attractive early-retirement offer, suspecting that it would only be a matter of time before you'd be put out to pasture. Maybe your company had a mandatory retirement age and you had to leave. Or maybe you saved enough money to retire at a relatively young age, thinking that you'd be happy to do nothing for the next thirty years. Whatever your reason for leaving, you now want back in. But as I'm sure many of you have found, big companies aren't in the market for an unretired executive seeking a top position at a top salary. If you're over age 55, you're even less attractive as a candidate.

Although you might strike out in your efforts to rejoin the corporate world, the entrepreneurial world beckons. What you may lack in youthful energy and unlimited time you more than make up for in experience, skills, and contacts. You probably also have more financial resources than younger ex-executives and have jettisoned the financial burdens that typically strain their budgets—chief among them, college education for the kids and mortgage payments.

You won't be the first retired executive to become a successful entrepreneur. Especially in the wake of corporate downsizings and associated early-retirement programs, more older executives are taking up new careers than ever before. Should you? Here's a scenario that might be instructive.

Rebirth

For thirty-three years, Alan Troy worked for a *Fortune* 500 company in various executive capacities. After a series of division vice-presidencies, he moved into a sales and marketing staff position, overseeing a number of divisional activities but without direct responsibility for any one division. He knew he was vulnerable, and when his company was taken over, Alan wasn't surprised at being offered an incentive-laden early-retirement package at age 58. He took it reluctantly; he wasn't ready to retire but saw the handwriting on the wall.

After a year of retirement, Alan was bored. He made a few stabs at returning to a corporate environment but had no luck. One day, he was out doing some yard work when a neighbor stopped by—a former owner of a local chain of hardware stores who had a proposition for Alan. The neighbor explained that he had signed an agreement with a German company to import a line of expensive tools; he needed a partner with sales experience to work with a broker group and sell the tools into stores. Would Alan be interested in a partnership in the new company?

Alan was. The deal was perfect: Alan didn't have to put up any money to become a partner, and his salary was based on a percentage of the profits. Although there wasn't much money at first, Alan was reenergized by the work. He loved the challenge of starting a new business and taking his old sales skills out of mothballs. Even better, he was successful at getting distribution, and the young tool company grew quickly, increasing the size of its staff, renting space in an office park, and adding another tool line from the German company. After two years, Alan was making more than he had at his former corporation and enjoyed more real responsibility than ever before.

His only problem was that he never quite got used to the small, entrepreneurial business. More than once, his partner had told him when he tried to implement a policy, "Alan, that's too corporate for us." Alan knew that was true, but he couldn't shake thirty-plus years of training. He sometimes worried that running the business by the seat of his pants wasn't in the business's best interests.

Then, another problem arose. Alan's partner, who was ten years his junior, decided that there was an opportunity for major expansion. He told Alan that he wanted to secure a bank loan to double their staff, greatly increase advertising expenditures, and add four new lines. Alan balked. He could envision the headaches such a move would cause and wasn't sure whether he was willing to commit to seeing all the changes through to completion. After all, he was 60 years old. Was he prepared to spend the next five years working ten-hour days trying to solve the irritating problems that seemed inevitable?

Reluctantly, he agreed to his partner's scheme. After two years, Alan had had enough. He was spending virtually every waking weekday hour either working or worrying about the business. Deciding that it wasn't worth it, Alan sold his interest in the business to his partner and retired for a second time.

Starting Over

Not all stories of unretirement end as Alan's did. But I relate it as a cautionary tale to illustrate the hazards of making an entrepreneurial move later in life. Although Alan enjoyed much of his entrepreneurial experience and contributed a great deal to his company's success, he wasn't prepared for the all-consuming entrepreneurial life-style.

I've found that certain factors greatly influence an unretired executive's success as an entrepreneur and his or her enjoyment of an entrepreneurial endeavor. Consider the following list:

Key Factors for a Successful Unretirement

- Your financial situation
- How much time you're willing to work
- Your attitude toward your former corporate job
- Recognition that things change and willingness to change with them

Your Financial Situation

By the time you retire, you've probably built up a nest egg for your retirement. If your entrepreneurial plans call for you to risk that nest egg on the business, you're risking a lot. Unlike a younger entrepreneur, you may not have the time or the energy to rebound from a failure; you may find yourself facing old age with all your savings gone. That possibility places enormous pressure on even the most vigorous individual, no matter his or her age. Such pressure can make even a successful enterprise a burden. Therefore, if money is tight, recognize that you're taking the ultimate entrepreneurial risk. If you've gone a lifetime without taking such a risk, it might be wise not to start now.

On the other hand, many unretired executives have a significant amount of "extra" cash to play with. If they lose that money, they might not be able to take the extended vacation they had planned, but their nest egg remains secure. In my experience, this is a far better situation than betting the bank on your entrepreneurial venture. You're able to take a reasonable risk. Better yet, your primary goal for your business might not be large profits. You have the luxury of a more intangible goal: deriving pleasure from finally being the boss of a business that involves doing something you enjoy. If success and concomitant wealth are the by-products, so much the better.

How Much Time You're Willing to Work

How much time are you willing to devote to being an entrepreneur? It's fine if you answer "Only two days a week" or "No more time than I spent on my corporate job." It's fine, at least, if you choose an enterprise that won't demand more time than you're prepared to give. I know a number of unretired, part-time entrepreneurs who are very happy—primarily consultants who pick and choose their assignments, turning down jobs that would force them to miss golf dates and weekends with grandchildren.

Remember, full-time entrepreneurial endeavors tend to require more time than corporate jobs. If you've spent decades following the standard corporate schedule—forty-hour weeks, regular nine-to-five workdays, three or four weeks of vacation—then you might be in for a shock. Of course, some unretired executives adjust very well to the new routine (or lack thereof). They have every intention of throwing themselves into their business and can't imagine anything better than wrapping their time up in their job.

The other issue is, How many years do you plan to work? Some entrepreneurial ventures take years of effort before they become profitable. Are you willing to wait? If not, either choose something that fits your timetable or pick a successor (often, a son or daughter) who will be able to carry on when you retire for good.

Your Attitude Toward Your Former Corporate Job

Did you hate your corporate job or love it? Were you forced out, or did you leave of your own volition? Are you becoming an entrepreneur because you're determined to show your former boss that there's life in your old bones yet or because you really want your own business?

Think about your years as a corporate executive and make a list of pluses and minuses. Be objective. Determine whether the list is weighted more positively or negatively. If you find you really disliked your corporate work, it doesn't necessarily mean you'll like entrepreneurial work—but it's a good possibility.

Attitudes become ingrained, and you have a lot of years as a manager behind you. Can you shed at least some of those attitudes? As the case of Alan Troy illustrates, many unretired entrepreneurs feel like fish out of water. Or they want to prove that they still have what it takes.

Interestingly, I've discovered that the unretired executives who make the best entrepreneurs are the sort of people who have always been open to new experiences: They love to travel to countries they've never visited before, take classes in subjects unrelated to their job, enjoy meeting people from all walks of life. If you possess this "open" attitude, great. And if you look back at your corporate years and realize that you really weren't very happy working for someone else, even better.

Recognition That Things Change and Willingness to Change With Them

Often, there's a gap of several years between an executive's retirement from the corporation and the beginning of his or her entrepreneurial venture. During this interim period, things change. New technological developments, business practices, and trends have all remade the work world in the ex-executive's absence. When such an individual becomes an entrepreneur, he or she is facing not only a new work style but a different work environment.

The combination of those two changes is a formidable obstacle. Old dogs can learn new tricks, but not always easily. I know of one product-sales executive who retired from his company and came back as a product-sales consultant after three years. To his dismay, he discovered that many of the processes had been transformed by technological advances during his absence from the work scene, and he was ignorant of the new methods. How adaptable are you? Are you willing to seek advice from someone half your age?

Furthermore, it's not only the tangible aspects of an industry that change but attitudes as well. When you were a vice-president, your corporate culture might have embraced a military code—with subordinates following orders unquestioningly. Now, your employees disdain such a code, frequently debating your commands. The more adaptable you are, the better. Even if you're a sole practitioner, and therefore don't have to deal with employees, you'll probably be interacting with clients, customers, partners, suppliers, etc. Many of them will be younger than you and accustomed to noncorporate modes of doing business. If you're rigid in your ideas, expect some friction—friction that won't bode well for your success or enjoyment of your new enterprise.

All Situations Are Special

Because there are so many special situations that it would be impossible to discuss all of them, this chapter has focused on those special situations that I believe executive-entrepreneurs are most likely to encounter. But to a certain extent, every situation is special. (Since executive-entrepreneurs are hybrids to begin with, how could it be otherwise?)

No matter how unique your situation, the one thing you can be sure of is that as an entrepreneur, you'll often find yourself in the midst of unfamiliar and unusual situations. It's part of the territory. Even though this chapter might not have discussed the specific entrepreneurial path you've chosen, it should have given you considerable insight into atypical entrepreneurial ventures in general. Armed with that insight, you'll be better-prepared to face the unfamiliar and unusual.

You should realize, however, that there's no such thing as being 100 percent prepared for an entrepreneurial venture. The best you'll be able to do is reduce the unfamiliar and unusual to manageable proportions. Ultimately, you must depend on your inherent or developed entrepreneurial qualities to help you adjust to your special circumstances.

FOUR

Transitional Tools

This final part of the book presents nuts-and-bolts information on such issues as financial planning, funding, taxes, structure, and employee benefits that every executive-entrepreneur faces in starting a business. Unlike a how-to manual on entrepreneurship, I haven't provided comprehensive information about each of these subjects. Instead, I've approached them from the narrow perspective of an executive-entrepreneur. For instance, how should your tax strategy change when you become an employer (rather than an employee)? Or what are your funding alternatives for your new business, and how can you use your executive background as leverage to secure funding?

These chapters provide a broad information base upon which you can build in a variety of ways. The best way is to consult the appropriate professionals—lawyers, accountants, bankers, and financial planners—who can help you with the specifics of everything from tax strategies to business plans.

Chapter 12

Financial Planning

The first step in creating a financial plan is to identify and organize the key elements of your financial life. Every asset, liability, income source, and expense has to be cataloged. That's the easy part. The hard part comes with the decision making: Which assets are going to be used for the new business? Which expenses are going to be eliminated to make room for the cost of the new enterprise? That this financial-planning process is crucial to the success of your venture is hardly an understatement. You must make your basic business and personal financial decisions at the beginning of your entrepreneurial career—you have to *plan* your finances. To plunge into a new business without such a plan is to invite failure.

Regardless of whether you've ever created a financial plan for yourself as an executive, the issues change when you become an entrepreneur, and your financial plan will therefore demand new priorities. When you were an executive, your financial planning was only marginally concerned with business. Now, it's the axis around which everything revolves. No longer is your financial plan designed to quadruple your assets. Instead, the goal is to stretch your assets, maintain your lifestyle, and facilitate your entrepreneurial success.

Getting Organized

How do you begin your plan? Start by filling out a worksheet such as the one at the end of this chapter. Starting on page 154 the relationship between the worksheet and your actual plan is discussed. First think about the information requested in the worksheet. If financial matters confuse you, don't worry. The process is relatively painless once you get yourself organized.

Organizing Your Assets

As you can see from the worksheet, you'll need to break your assets into a variety of categories. Before you do so, however, consider these two questions:

  1. How easy will it be to turn a given asset into cash?
  2. Would you be willing to turn a given asset into cash?

For instance, your house is worth $300,000. Obviously, selling your house isn't the only way you can get at that $300,000. Many executives, prior to becoming entrepreneurs, ask their bank for an equity loan on their house to establish a line of credit or refinance their mortgage to free up the house's equity. This doesn't mean you have to use the money for your entrepreneurial business. But it does make that asset—or part of it—available to you.

If you're going to establish a line of credit, it's wise to do it before starting your business. Obtaining an equity loan takes time, and you might require cash immediately if your business experiences a downturn. Also, you'll probably be in a better financial position to secure an equity loan while you're still a corporate employee.

Look at your stocks. Are they easily salable? Certainly, you can sell New York Stock Exchange securities, but you don't know exactly what you'll get for them at an undetermined point in the future. Other stocks might not translate into cash. Stock in a closely held company, for instance, might not be liquid. Therefore, you'll need to divide your assets into two categories: those that you can quickly turn into cash and those that you cannot liquidate.

Next, determine which assets you won't liquidate under any circumstances. Such assets might include money you're reserving for some other purpose, like retirement or your children's education, or valuables like your wife's jewelry or your husband's art collection. This category of assets should be untouchable or, at the very least, usable only under extreme financial duress.

Organizing Your Expenses

Divide your expenses into two categories: fixed and discretionary. Fixed expenses are relatively unavoidable outlays such as rent or mortgage payments, utility bills, college tuition, and so on. Discretionary expenses, on the other hand, are outlays that increase and decrease as you change your life-style—for example, money spent on restaurants, clothing, vacations.

After you've made your list, figure out how much money is flowing from your bank account weekly, not only for each individual expense but as a total for both categories. This will give you an estimate of what you spend—and on what you spend it—each week. Remember, though, that this is an approximation. Everyone has surprises, such as a leaky roof or a stalled car, that will change the total.

Organizing Your Income

Finally, list your income. Although your salary will have stopped if you've already left your corporation, you probably have other sources of income: interest on savings, stock dividends, severance payments, money from rental properties, and so on. Take a long, hard look at these income sources. As an entrepreneur, you are about to assume a significant risk by starting a new business. You don't need additional risks, such as chancy stock holdings or real estate deals.

Other Planning Issues

When you make the transition from executive to entrepreneur, many other areas of your life are affected besides purely financial matters. Upon leaving the corporation, you'll find yourself without various types of insurance—medical, dental, life, long-term disability. Your financial plan should take insurance and other issues into consideration, including wills, trusts, and estate planning. This is especially important if you have a family. Without the shelter of a corporate benefits package, you leave yourself and your family at risk. A good financial plan analyzes each of these areas and provides you with strategies and tactics to protect your family based on anticipated and unanticipated future events.

Choosing a Financial Planner

Although anyone can create a financial plan on his or her own, it is wise to seek professional assistance to ensure that it is the right plan. A financial planner is in the best position to interpret the data described earlier, recommend courses of action, implement them, and monitor the results. Choosing a financial planner is similar to choosing an accountant (or any other professional financial adviser): There are a lot of planners out there, and you have to learn to separate the wheat from the chaff.

Your first resource in this selection process could be your former employer. Increasingly, corporations are employing outside financial planners for their employees, either as a perk for executives or during the outplacement process. You might have worked with one if you went through outplacement, and if you were pleased with his or her services, you might want to continue using that individual. If not, here are some factors to consider in searching for a planner:

- What is the planner's track record? Has he or she worked with other companies you've heard about? Has the planner helped other entrepreneurs in your situation? Will he or she provide you with a list of references?
- Is the financial planner part of a larger organization? If so, that's often to your advantage. If he or she is associated with a group of other professionals—certified public accountants, attorneys, actuaries, chartered life underwriters—you will have access to specialists who are integral to the planning process.
- Is the financial fee relatively low? Some financial planners generally provide their service for a fee that reflects only a portion of the time they invest in creating a plan. Most who charge low fees also sell products: insurance, investments, etc. They hope that their financial-planning

clients will purchase one or more of those products from them, for which they'll receive a commission. Financial planners who do not rely on commissions naturally have to charge a much higher fee to cover their time and expertise.

Factors to Consider Before Planning

When you sit down to map out your financial plan, be prepared for a shock. Unless you're in the rare and enviable position of having a sizable amount of money saved for your entrepreneurial endeavor, you must change your perspective on financial issues—how you look at salary, discretionary income, and investments.

Don't expect this perspective shift to be easy. For a significant period of time, you've been operating within well-defined financial parameters. As a corporate executive, you could estimate your yearly income with accuracy. In addition, your business expenses were nil. All that has now changed. Rethink your expenses, investments, and income with the following factors in mind:

1. Reduce your discretionary expenses to make your business dollars last longer. You're buying time, crucial to any budding entrepreneur. There are obvious areas where you can cut expenses: vacations, dining out, new cars, and so on. But don't go overboard. I've seen too many entrepreneurs try to pare their expenses to the bone, much to the chagrin and anger of their families. You'll have to strike a compromise between your business's and family's requirements. You'll need your family's support and encouragement, and if they feel they're suffering because of radical expense cutting, you may find the situation impossible.

2. Expect to receive far less compensation in salary than you did with your former employer. When you draw up a pro forma, you'll have to decide on your salary, and you'll be tempted to award yourself handsome compensation. After all, being able to dictate your own salary terms is a heady feeling,

and you'll want to capitalize on it. Don't! Be conservative. If you estimate your business's first-year revenue at $100,000, don't give yourself an $80,000 salary. You'll lack a sufficient cushion. During the first months of any business, cash is tight. You'll quickly discover the difference between income and cash flow. It might be advisable to forsake any salary during the first six months, accruing you salary and taking it only when the cash is in hand. Your salary should be flexible, and you'd be wise to take advantage of that flexibility.

Even if you're receiving a sizable loan from a bank or a tidy sum from a venture-capital group, don't get greedy and assign a large percentage of it for your salary. Entrepreneurs learn that sound cash management means keeping your debt as low as possible; you want the bank or venture-capital group to own as little of your business as possible.

3. Change your approach to investing. Many of you have invested in stocks for appreciation over time. If you're strapped for cash, it's wise to discontinue this practice. Investment for appreciation generally involves the greatest risk of loss, and that's the last thing you want to happen when you're starting your business.

Now I'll move on to the practical tool I mentioned earlier in the chapter for gathering financial information, the financial-planning worksheet.

Your Financial Plan

As you start to fill out the worksheet, you will find that certain questions key into important financial-planning issues. These should be answered with care and reflection since they will have the greatest impact on the final plan. Here are some of the most meaningful issues.

Termination and Other Pay

The estimated starting or payment date of any termination and severance or other pay can have a significant impact on your taxes. In your calendar year of termination, it is likely that you will have a greater than normal income (and hence owe more in taxes). Here are some examples of taxable income you may receive in addition to your regular salary:

Severance pay
Unused vacation
Unused sick leave
Accrued bonus

The result of these extra payments would place you in a higher tax bracket. Since it's likely that your first year as an entrepreneur will produce less than normal income, explore the possibility of deferring these extra payments until the start of the new year. Good timing may allow you to keep more of these funds.

Group Insurance Benefits

Whether you leave the corporation on your own or because you are a casualty of downsizing, you may continue your group medical insurance under the Consolidated Omnibus Budget Reconciliation Act of 1986 (COBRA). However, continuation is at your expense, so do check on alternative individual or family plans. A nongroup plan could be significantly less costly (for more information on benefits, see Chapter 15). Be careful to maintain your old group coverage until the new policy is actually issued. Of course, qualifying for coverage under your spouse's group plan, if possible, could be the best solution.

Qualified Retirement Plans

The wealth you have accumulated in your qualified retirement plan may well be your best (and largest) investment. As a rule, these are the funds you should touch last. Money in a qualified plan is largely tax-deductible; however as soon as you remove the money, it becomes subject to federal and state income taxes and could shrink by as much as 40 percent. In addition, if you are under age 57½, it could be subject to a 10 percent penalty, increasing the possible shrinkage to 50 percent! Remember, this money grows tax-free in the plan, and most investment yields outside the plan will be taxable. Opt to utilize other funds first in your entrepreneurial venture, and tag these funds for emergency use only.

Deferred Compensation

If you have a deferred compensation arrangement that does not fall into the class of qualified plans, chances are the funds in it will not enjoy tax-deductible status, as do funds in the qualified plans. The money will also be subject to income taxes when you do receive it. Hence these funds should be treated in the same way as severance pay and deferred, if possible, until a year when your other income is less.

Assets and Liabilities

Residences

The value of primary and secondary residences will be very meaningful in your financial plan. Equity in these homes could provide you with cash in the form of a home equity loan and/or collateral for a bank loan. Any bank considering a loan to your new enterprise will look at your assets as collateral (see Chapter 13). Refinancing your mortgage is also a method to free up equity and reduce monthly payments.

Securities

The value of most securities is tied to a market so cashing out of your favorite stock when the market is at a low point is no fun for the pocketbook or the ego. Still, if your goal is a successful business and you need cash, it is better to cash in the securities than to forgo the enterprise or cash in the qualified plan money. The best approach is to use your securities as part of your collateral against a loan—that way you have your stock and your cash. But remember that the worksheet also deals with liabilities and interest payments. Bank loans produce debt service—the interest and principal the bank will be looking for as loan repayment. Look at those securities again. Will they go up in value enough to pay the interest charges a bank loan will generate?

Discretionary Expenses

This is obviously the area with the most elasticity. Vacations, charitable contributions, and entertainment could be considered a total waste to the entrepreneur with a budding business. Still, as I've said before, if you have a family, remember that family members generally don't have the excitement of the new establishment to buoy them up. Finding less expensive types of entertainment might keep up your family's spirits while holding down spending. Certainly, items such as home improvements and investments should be avoided when starting your new business.

Life Insurance

If you have permanent life insurance (whole life or universal life), you may have cash values in the policies that you can borrow out on. This money could be a source of extra cash, or you can use it to make premium payments and reduce expenses. Often, insurance policy loans carry a lower interest rate than commerical (bank) loans. Although a policy loan reduces the death benefit, in theory you have the cash elsewhere, so the reduced death benefit plus the cash amounts to the same level of protection.

In building your financial plan, the idea is to look at each asset and liability, each income and expense item, in a new light. Ask yourself, "How can I manipulate this to increase my income or reduce my expense or free up some cash?" Remember, the goal of the plan is to increase the odds of your business succeeding while selecting those expenses and assets that are essential to your and your family's continued well-being. The worksheet and your good judgment will begin that process.

Financial-Planning Worksheet

The decision to become an entrepreneur will demand close scrutiny of your present financial position and real planning to enable you to stretch your assets so that you can start your new business and still maintain your life-style. Starting a new business without a financial plan, however, is like sailing to Hawaii without a set of charts. You are much more likely to arrive safely if you know where you are at each stage of the journey.

The first step in preparing a financial plan is to find and organize the information that will be required to properly complete the plan. This worksheet has been designed to help you compile that information. Doing so will enable you to answer the question "How much am I worth?" More important, it will enable you to start objectively analyzing your income, assets, liabilities, and expenses.

I recommend that you complete the entire worksheet, since this will allow you or your financial planner to prepare a more accurate financial plan.

In addition to completing the worksheet, you should compile the following data, which will be helpful in preparing your financial plan:

1. Your most recent federal and state income-tax returns.
2. Your most recent wills and any trust documents that have been prepared for you and your spouse.
3. Any insurance policies on your life and your spouse's life.
4. Brokerage or investment statements.
5. Relevant information on any tax shelters, such as a prospectus or income/loss projection.
6. Financial statements for any personally owned family or other business interests you may have.
7. Your most recent employee-benefits statement showing any account balances for profit-sharing plans, stock-option plans, and other deferred-compensation plans, both qualified and nonqualified. Employee-benefits handbooks, if available, would also be helpful.

PERSONAL INFORMATION

Telephone (_____) _____

Name

ENTREPRENEUR _____

SPOUSE _____

Address _____

_____

Date of birth

ENTREPRENEUR _____/_____/_____   SPOUSE _____/_____/_____

COMPENSATION INFORMATION

ENTREPRENEUR

Employer _____

Scheduled annual
compensation $ _____   Bonus $ _____

Termination pay $ _____

☐ Lump sum $ _____   Estimated payment date ___/___/___

☐ Other method (specify) _____

Amount $ _____

Starting date ___/___/___
Ending date ___/___/___

SPOUSE

Scheduled annual
compensation $ _____   Bonus $ _____

BUSINESS BENEFITS AND RETIREMENT PLANS

CLIENT

Group Insurance Benefits

	Cost of Coverage	Date Coverage Expires
Group life	$ _____	__/__/__
Group medical	$ _____	__/__/__
Miscellaneous	$ _____	__/__/__

Qualified Retirement Plan(s)

	Current Amount	Distribution Options and When Available	Ownership (H/W/J)[1]
Profit sharing	$ _____	_____	_____
401(k)/CODA[2]	$ _____	_____	_____
Thrift	$ _____	_____	_____
ESOP[3]	$ _____	_____	_____
IRA	$ _____	_____	_____
Pension(s)	$ _____	_____	_____
☐ Lump sum	$ _____	Earliest available __/__/__	
☐ Monthly benefit	$ _____	Earliest available __/__/__	

1. H = husband; W = wife; J = joint
2. CODA = Cash or deferred arrangement
3. ESOP = employee stock-ownership plan

Deferred Compensation

Description	Benefit	Frequency	Date Available	Other Benefits
_____	_____	_____	___/___/___	_____
_____	_____	_____	___/___/___	_____
_____	_____	_____	___/___/___	_____

Alternative Coverage

Will you be covered by your spouse's group-insurance benefits, retirement plans, or other employee benefits during your period of unemployment? ☐ Yes ☐ No

If yes, please describe briefly.

_____

_____

_____

Stock Options

Description	Number of Shares	Grant Date	Expiration Date	Exercise Price	Type (ISO NQ)[1]
_____	_____	___/___/___	___/___/___	$_____	_____
_____	_____	___/___/___	___/___/___	$_____	_____
_____	_____	___/___/___	___/___/___	$_____	_____
_____	_____	___/___/___	___/___/___	$_____	_____

Planned Retirement Date ___/___/___

1. ISO = incentive stock option; NQ = nonqualified

ASSETS AND LIABILITIES

Personal Assets

	Current Value	Ownership (H/W/J)	Related Liability	Origination Date	Original Balance	Term	Interest Rate
Residence (primary)	$ _____	_____	$ _____	___/___/___	$ _____	$ _____	_____ %
Residence (secondary)	$ _____	_____	$ _____	___/___/___	$ _____	$ _____	_____ %
Automobile	$ _____	_____	$ _____	___/___/___	$ _____	$ _____	_____ %
Automobile	$ _____	_____	$ _____	___/___/___	$ _____	$ _____	_____ %
Furniture	$ _____	_____	$ _____	___/___/___	$ _____	$ _____	_____ %
Collectibles	$ _____	_____	$ _____	___/___/___	$ _____	$ _____	_____ %
Other	$ _____	_____	$ _____	___/___/___	$ _____	$ _____	_____ %

Year in which automobiles will be replaced _____

Securities (bonds, notes, nontaxable)

Description	Number of Shares	Cost	Purchase Date	Current Value	Annual Income	Ownership (H/W/J)
_____	_____	$ _____	__/__/__	$ _____	$ _____	_____
_____	_____	$ _____	__/__/__	$ _____	$ _____	_____
_____	_____	$ _____	__/__/__	$ _____	$ _____	_____
_____	_____	$ _____	__/__/__	$ _____	$ _____	_____
Cash/checking				$ _____	$ _____	_____
Savings/money market				$ _____	$ _____	_____

Real Estate (apartments, land, etc.)

Description	Current Value	Cost	Purchase Date	Annual Cash Flow	Ownership (H/W/J)
_____	$ _____	$ _____	__/__/__	$ _____	_____
_____	$ _____	$ _____	__/__/__	$ _____	_____
_____	$ _____	$ _____	__/__/__	$ _____	_____

Other Investments (partnerships, etc.)

Description	Current Value	Cost	Purchase Date	Annual Cash Flow	Ownership (H/W/J)
_____	$ ____	$ ____	__/__/__	$ ____	_____
_____	$ ____	$ ____	__/__/__	$ ____	_____
_____	$ ____	$ ____	__/__/__	$ ____	_____

Other Liabilities

Description	Original Date	Original Amount	Term	Interest Rate	Current Liability	Ownership (H/W/J)
_____	__/__/__	$ ____	____	____ %	$ ____	_____
_____	__/__/__	$ ____	____	____ %	$ ____	_____
_____	__/__/__	$ ____	____	____ %	$ ____	_____

Other Income (alimony, business income, rents, etc.)

_____

ANNUAL EXPENSES/DISBURSEMENTS

Fixed Expenses

Housing

Mortgage payments	$ _____	Property tax	$ _____
Homeowner's insurance	$ _____	Maintenance	$ _____

Transportation

Auto loans	$ _____	Gas, oil, repairs	$ _____
Other	$ _____		

Education

Private school/ college	$ _____	Other

Insurance

Medical	$ _____	Life	$ _____
Disability	$ _____	Other	

Other Fixed

Food	$ _____	Cleaning	$ _____
Telephone	$ _____	Medical care—not covered	$ _____

Fixed Expenses, con't.

Prescriptions—not covered	$ ———	
Taxes—deductible	$ ———	
Support of dependents	$ ———	
Loan and charge accounts	$ ———	
Alimony	$ ———	
Miscellaneous	$ ———	
Taxes—nondeductible	$ ———	
Other—nondeductible	$ ———	

Total Fixed Expenses $ ———

Discretionary Expenses

Entertainment	$ ———	
Gifts	$ ———	
Retirement plans	$ ———	
Other—nondeductible	$ ———	
Vacation/recreation	$ ———	
Hobbies	$ ———	
IRA	$ ———	
Miscellaneous purchases	$ ———	
Charitable	$ ———	
Home improvement	$ ———	
Other—deductible	$ ———	
Miscellaneous	$ ———	

Total Discretionary Expenses $ ———

Other Notes and Comments

_____

_____

EDUCATION PLANNING

Child/Current Age	Public or Private College	Estimated Annual Cost in Today's Dollars	Number of Years	Other	Number of Years
_____	_____	$ _____	$ _____	_____	$ _____
_____	_____	$ _____	$ _____	_____	$ _____
_____	_____	$ _____	$ _____	_____	$ _____
_____	_____	$ _____	$ _____	_____	$ _____

LIFE INSURANCE

Policy	Type	Insured	Owner	Beneficiary	Face Value	Cash Value (Net of Loans)	Annual Premium
_____	_____	_____	_____	_____	$ _____	$ _____	$ _____
_____	_____	_____	_____	_____	$ _____	$ _____	$ _____
_____	_____	_____	_____	_____	$ _____	$ _____	$ _____
_____	_____	_____	_____	_____	$ _____	$ _____	$ _____
_____	_____	_____	_____	_____	$ _____	$ _____	$ _____
_____	_____	_____	_____	_____	$ _____	$ _____	$ _____

ESTATE PLANNING

Do you and your spouse have wills? ☐ Yes ☐ No   Do you and your spouse have trusts? ☐ Yes ☐ No   If yes, please describe and note the date the documents were executed.

_____

_____

_____

Are you or any member of your family the beneficiary of a trust? ☐ Yes ☐ No   If yes, please describe.

_____

_____

_____

Please provide any other relevant information about your estate situation (potential inheritance, specific bequests).

_____

_____

Chapter 13
Funding

Funding an entrepreneurial business is similar to drilling for oil: The oil is out there, but it lies deep and you have to know where to sink your well. Executives leaving large organizations generally have better equipment for "drilling" than other entrepreneurs. As you'll see, your asset monies combined with your track record as an executive will serve you well.

On the negative side, many of you aren't accustomed to securing funding. When you needed money for a corporate project, there was a formal procedure you could follow: It was a matter of stating your case verbally and in writing, getting approvals, and fighting for budgetary allocations. Finding money outside of the corporation isn't such a cut-and-dried process. Not only are there a number of funding sources to choose from, but there are a variety of ways to approach those sources.

Further complicating matters is the way funding affects your personal life-style. No longer can you separate business from personal expenses. A dollar spent on business is a dollar taken away from your mortgage. In fact, before you even start thinking about business money, you have to examine your personal cash-flow requirements. If you completed the worksheet at the end of Chapter 12, you probably already have some idea of your needs.

How Much Do You Need, and for How Long?

Every new entrepreneur is under various types of pressure, and financial pressure is often the most severe. Coping with that pressure is especially difficult when it affects both your personal and business finances. Therefore, the first funding issue is personal. Think of yourself as someone who is going to Las Vegas. You walk up to the craps table with your fortune in your pocket, but you say to yourself, "I'm only willing to lose so much and no more."

Before you become an entrepreneur, determine how much you're going to set aside for personal use. The way to make that determination is to figure out how much money you and your family will need to maintain a given life-style for a two-year period (Chapter 12, "Financial Planning," details how to calculate that amount). Make a vow not to invest any of that money in your business. That way, no matter what happens with your venture, your personal finances will have a two-year safety net.

Estimating Start-Up Costs

How can you estimate your start-up costs? The logical way to begin is to find people who have done the same thing you plan to do. As long as they're not direct competitors of your new enterprise, others will be willing to help. You'll find that most people enjoy sharing information about their success, including general information about budgets. And in contrast to the situation in the corporate world, in the entrepreneurial world, the decision to share information can be made by just a few people. Furthermore, entrepreneurs tend to want to assist other entrepreneurs.

Another source of information is suppliers. If you plan to open a restaurant, a kitchen-supplies vendor will probably have a great deal of information about the anticipated and unanticipated costs your business will face.

Also contact the appropriate trade association. Virtually every field of business has one, and that association has probably compiled numerous relevant statistics, including financial facts and figures. The association will be glad to help you, especially if you become a member.

Once you've done all that, make a list of your anticipated costs and total all the numbers. Whatever amount you come up with, add 25 percent. Estimates are invariably low. Unexpected expenses almost always arise, no matter what your business might be. The extra 25 percent will provide you with a needed cushion.

Funding Sources

Let's assume you require $500,000 to get your business off the ground and keep it running for one year. How do you start rounding up the money? Here are the sources you can tap: your own assets (including any funds due you as a result of your termination); lenders (such as banks); friends and associates; venture-capital groups; Small Business Administration (SBA) loans; and federal, state, and private loans and grants. These are the sources most executives-turned-entrepreneurs use. There are other possibilities, such as participating in a leveraged buyout or an initial public offering, but because most of you aren't in a position to take advantage of LBO or IPO, I'll confine the following discussion to the typical sources.

No matter which funding source you target, you should have certain key information in hand before approaching that source. Figure 13-1 shows the information requested by virtually every type of funding source, and the faster your provide this information, the faster you'll receive the money you need.

Bank Loans

You will risk your time, energy, career, and many other things in your quest to become a successful entrepreneur. But if your new business requires $100,000 and you have exactly that sum in your bank account, it isn't wise to leave yourself with a zero-sum balance. Instead, share the risk with a lender. For most of you, that lender will be a bank.

Which bank should you choose to be your lender? Ideally, it will be a bank with which you have a prior relationship. A bank in the community where your business will be located is also a good prospect. That prior relationship is more important than you might think. Even if you only have a checking account with a bank, that counts for something in the eyes of the

Figure 13-1. Funding checklist.

> ▸ Background on yourself—stressing your corporate accomplishments, especially those that seem applicable to your new venture.
>
> ▸ Amount of money you wish to borrow.
>
> ▸ How you plan to use the borrowed funds. Your repayment plan—how long it will take and where you plan to get the money.
>
> ▸ Whether there are others who will be partners or part owners, and whether you will be receiving loans from other sources.
>
> ▸ How you will structure the venture—corporation, sole proprietorship, partnership.
>
> ▸ What type of venture it is—retail, consulting, etc.
>
> ▸ Description of the products or services you'll offer.
>
> ▸ A business plan, including financial projections.

lender; it will be more favorably disposed to grant a loan to you than to someone without a prior relationship. Community ties are important because banks have a mandate to serve their communities; given a choice, they would rather fund a business in the neighborhood than one somewhere else. Furthermore, don't discount the "people" aspect of lending. If you want to open a restaurant for businesspeople and the loan officer feels that the neighborhood doesn't have a good place for lunch, it will influence his or her decision.

Other factors will also influence a bank's lending decision. Look over the following list to determine where you'll stand when you approach a bank for money:

> ▸ *Size of loan:* It's said to be easier to borrow $10 million than $10,000. There's some logic behind that statement, in as much as a bank charges points for a loan (each point is one percent of the loan amount), and the larger the loan, the more money the bank makes. Still, small,

community banks make small, community loans. Don't ask for more than you need on the assumption that doing so will improve your chances of getting the loan.

▸ *Your credentials:* As a former executive with a sizable corporation, your track record will impress bank officials. If your proposed business is related to what you did at the corporation, the bank will be even more impressed.

▸ *Collateral:* What assets can you pledge in case your business goes under and you can't repay the loan? If your assets equal or are close to the loan amount, that will greatly facilitate the process. As a general rule, banks expect borrowers to risk some or all of their personal assets.

▸ *Business plan:* You've probably done this type of plan— or a variation of it—for corporate projects. Make your plan professional, convincing, and above all else, realistic; don't exaggerate revenue expectations. Bankers have seen hundreds of these plans, and they know how to spot hype.

▸ *Type of loan:* Another important issue is the type of loan you're requesting. There are four types: seasonal, working capital, term, and interim.

1. A seasonal loan is more likely to be used by an established business with a known history. It's designed to help you through a slow period in your business cycle, when expenditures must be made and cash flow is slow.

2. Working-capital loans, as the name implies, are permanent loans (usually, for one to seven years) used to provide cash for general business needs.

3. Term loans help finance equipment, fixtures, or facilities, and they can also help provide working capital. A term loan is for a specific period of time.

4. Interim loans, also called bridge loans, are for short periods of time and are repaid through financing, refinancing, sales of assets, or money from other sources.

One thing you can do to make your guarantee a bit more palatable is to restructure your assets before approaching the bank. For instance, it might be wise to put your house in joint tenancy with your spouse. Because you sign the loan and not your spouse, if you default, the bank is only entitled to your half of the house. You can do the same thing with other assets, putting trusts in your children's names, for instance. There's nothing illegal about any of this. You do, of course, have to acknowledge to the bank what assets are in your spouse's and children's names. But this restructuring does provide you with some reassurance that everything you own won't go down the drain if you can't repay the loan. It will, however, reduce the amount of collateral you have and therefore may reduce the size of the loan you can get.

Finally, approach banks as a seller, not a buyer. When you were with the corporation, the roles were reversed. Your corporate bank treated your company as the wealthy and privileged customer it is. If your company wanted a loan, and it was financially healthy, the bank generally responded, "How much?" As an entrepreneur, you have to sell the bank. To do so, arm yourself with all the facts you can muster about your proposed venture. If your financials are in order, if you're asking for an appropriate amount of money, if your business concept makes sense, and if you demonstrate an ability to make good on the loan, you should receive what you're asking for.

SBA Loans

If banks tell you that your loan is too "risky," you may want to try the SBA route. The Small Business Administration tends to make somewhat more risky loans. The trade-off is a slightly higher interest rate—usually, around 2.5 percent over prime.

SBA leading officers evaluate your loan request in much the same manner as a bank officer. You'll need to make a strong argument for your proposed venture in writing. Unlike a bank, however, the SBA is less concerned with your collateral than with your financial projections, your managerial ability, and your equity in the venture.

The SBA also guarantees loans. You may be able to get a bank loan if the SBA is willing to guarantee it (the SBA guarantees up to 90 percent of the amount loaned). A bank officer can act as an intermediary between you and the SBA, or you can deal with the SBA directly.

Venture Capital

Venture capital can be defined in many ways. It can be money put up by a venture-capital group, by a syndicate of investors, or by a father-in-law. Whatever the source, the people putting up the cash will want something sizable in exchange—generally, a piece of the business.

As an executive yearning for the freedom of your own enterprise, this might be a difficult concept to accept. From a philosophical standpoint, you're accountable to someone besides yourself. From a practical standpoint, you find yourself doing all the work yet sharing the rewards with someone who is contributing little or nothing to the business besides dollars.

Many executives-turned-entrepreneurs therefore try for a compromise. They obtain the bulk of their start-up money via a bank loan and supplement that with additional funding from a venture-capital source. In this way, the venture-capital group (or individual) has a smaller piece of the action and less of a say in how they run their business. If the business is successful, it's easier to buy out the venture capitalist's share if he or she only owns a relatively small percentage.

Where do you find venture capital? The following are likely candidates: (1) a venture-capital group; (2) the venture-capital arm of a brokerage house or other financial institution; and (3) friends, relatives, or former business associates with money to invest.

Venture-capital groups run the gamut, from professional, well-managed, ethical organizations to those that are just the opposite. Before striking a deal with one, learn something about it. For instance:

- What other deals has the group done? Have you heard of any of the companies, and can you contact any of them

to determine the relationship between the venture organization and the entrepreneur?

‣ Has the venture group done deals similar to yours? Does
it have valuable expertise that it can contribute beyond
its dollars?
‣ What are the terms of the proposed agreement? Some
venture-capital groups charge fees; they shouldn't. If a
venture organization suggests such fees to you, be wary
of it.

Shop around and negotiate. Don't go to a venture-capital
group on bended knee. Use the negotiation skills you acquired
as an executive. The organization that initially wants 50 percent of your business might be willing to settle for a smaller
percentage if you present a strong case.

Venture-capital groups associated with brokerage houses
have created a venture-capital pool; the venture-capital arm
then looks for appropriate investments for that pool of offer-
ings. In most cases, though, these organizations are looking for
major investments; they're not usually attracted to one-person
operations. Unless you require a substantial amount of money,
this might not be the best route for you.

The final approach to securing venture-capital funding is
to create a syndicate of investors, consisting of anyone you
choose. Before passage of the 1986 Tax Reform Act, limited
partnerships were popular because of the tax breaks that
partnerships received. Now, the tax incentives are no longer
there. Still, don't overlook this possibility. If the prime rate is
low and investments aren't paying what they used to, you
might be able to convince others that your business will yield
a superior return. Tap your contacts in the corporate world;
you're likely to find more than one executive who wants to
participate "vicariously" in an entrepreneurial venture.

Brokered Capital

Executives looking for alternative sources of funding—especially if they don't require seven-figure sums—should investigate the growing number of capital-resources organizations,

often part of employee-benefits companies. Many times, these organizations represent clients who are looking for ways to invest capital—either pension-fund monies or excess cash.

Generally, these organizations are skilled at linking two or more interested parties. Not only can they assist in raising capital, but they are knowledgeable about designing tax and business strategies that can increase a fledgling company's chances for success.

Government and Foundation Loans and Grants

Depending on your business, you could be eligible for state, federal, or private loans and grants. To qualify, you must meet a number of requirements. For instance, you're most likely to get a state loan if your business will bring a sizable number of new jobs to the state. For certain types of loans, it also helps to be a member of a minority group. Many foundations are set up to provide grants for a particular industry: high-tech, medical research, etc.

These loans and grants are fine if you meet the requirements. Be prepared, however, for a great deal of paperwork and red tape. Also be prepared to wait: Bureaucracies move slowly, and it could take a year or longer to receive the money after you fill out the forms.

If you're dealing with the state, its assistance might not take the form of cash. Instead, it might be willing to give you other incentives to locate in a given area, such as granting tax breaks or providing office space.

Corporate Support

As you probably know, corporations provide financial and other assistance to entrepreneurial ventures that will directly benefit their organization. They do so because they want to reap the rewards of the project before the competition does. They might even insist on a contract under which they receive exclusive rights to the venture's product. In many instances, corporate-entrepreneur projects involve some sort of new technology.

If you're considering this route, approach a prospective company through the relevant department rather than via the financial division. Although your proposal will ultimately end up with a corporate finance executive, you need to acquire an advocate within the company. If, for instance, you plan to develop new MIS systems, contact an MIS executive about your project. He or she will know how to evaluate your business and determine how it will benefit the corporation.

Ex-executives should be aware, however, of the negatives of working with a corporation. Whether it's your former company or another one, you will find yourself indebted to a corporate entity. That means you might be laboring under the same sort of scrutiny and restrictions as when you were employed by a large organization.

It comes down to a trade-off. If you're willing to sacrifice some of your entrepreneurial freedom for corporate sponsorship, fine. You might want to regard your initial corporate linkage as a launching pad, a temporary alliance designed to get your business off the ground.

Termination Package

When you leave a corporation, you'll receive a variety of monies (or promises of sums at a future date), including severance pay and vacation pay as well as funds from such programs as pension plans, profit-sharing plans, stock-option plans, corporate thrift, and 401(k). Benefits and compensation can be divided into two categories: qualified and nonqualified. The nonqualified sums—vacation pay, severance, etc.—arrive as cash. The qualified dollars you may or may not receive as cash.

One thing to keep in mind before deciding whether to take the cash is taxes. If, for example, you have $200,000 due you in profit-sharing money—in addition to $100,000 in severance, vacation, and other nonqualified compensation—you'll be taxed heavily on such a large sum. Therefore, it might be in your best interests to defer receipt of the money to a time when you'll be in a lower tax bracket. Also, there's a 10 percent penalty for taking certain types of benefits, such as 401(k)'s, early (generally before age 55).

Still, don't underestimate the value of your benefits and compensation package. If you're a top executive who's been downsized out of a job, you may receive six figures' worth of severance and other nonqualified money. Or you might be lucky enough to be able to receive your profit-sharing funds at the beginning of a year during which you don't foresee much income from your new business; in this case, you might be in a low enough tax bracket that it would be advisable to take the money.

Chapter 14
Structure and Taxation

Any discussion of taxes is at best dangerous because of the speed with which tax laws change. As a new entrepreneur, it's essential that you deal with professionals, both legal and accounting, when considering any decision concerning the structure of your business or the tax impact of various strategies. One aspect of the commitment that you must make to your business is the willingness to spend some funds on expert advice, and few types of advice are more important than adequate legal and accounting services. Profits come in many forms, and a dollar of taxes saved is worth more than a dollar of profit earned by the corporation. You would be foolish to build a successful business and then dissipate its assets by failing to get adequate legal and tax guidance.

One of the decisions you'll be faced with upon becoming an entrepreneur involves what legal form your business will take. There are three general types of businesses:

1. *Sole proprietorship:* a business owned by an individual
2. *Partnership:* a business owned by two or more individuals
3. *Corporation:* an entity unto itself that may be owned by one or more individuals

Needless to say, lawyers and accountants could produce voluminous explanations detailing the nature and background of the differences between these three business forms. For our purpose, though, the most important differences involve liability and taxation.

From a liability standpoint, a sole proprietorship or partnership is you. That is, if a sole proprietor or partnership borrows money, enters into contracts, or gets sued, you your-

185

self, as the sole proprietor (owner) or partner in that business, becomes liable for all of its debts. If the business were a corporation, however, your liability would be limited to whatever investment you had made in that corporation. For example, if you invested $10,000 in a sole proprietorship and that business were sued for $100,000, the plaintiff in the suit (i.e., the person doing the suing) could collect $100,000 from the business (assuming it had the funds), or $10,000 from the business and $90,000 from you as its owner. In the same situation, were the business a corporation with $10,000 in assets, the plaintiff could collect $10,000 from the business and nothing from you. The corporation would act as a shield limiting liability. Of course, this is an oversimplification. As an officer of the corporation, you could carry some liability for malfeasance or negligence that might result in your becoming personally liable. As a general rule, however, the corporation can stand as a barrier between you and a plaintiff looking for damages.

The second difference between these business forms involves taxation. A sole proprietorship or partnership effectively passes all of its income back to the owner(s) of the company, and that income gets taxed at the tax rate(s) of the individual(s) involved. For example, if your sole proprietorship earned $10,000 after all expenses, that $10,000 would show up on your tax return as income and be taxed at your tax rate. Currently, the highest individual federal income tax rate is 31 percent. The corporate tax rate is as high as 34 percent. Although it's conceivable that a corporation could pay a higher tax rate than an individual, there are techniques that can mitigate that difference.

There are two types of corporations: a "C," or regular, corporation and an "S" corporation (so called because it is formed under Subchapter S of the Internal Revenue Code). An "S" corporation is taxed like a sole proprietorship or partnership. Were your corporation to make a Subchapter S election, any profits earned by the corporation would pass through the corporation and show up on your tax return as income, taxed at your individual tax rate as opposed to a corporate tax rate. That means you could elect to have a corporate form of business for its liability shield but still effectively pay taxes as an individual—the best of both worlds.

In deciding what form your business should take, perhaps you should start by considering the nature of the business. If your proposed venture has significant liability potential, the corporate form might be the natural choice in order to provide you with a liability shield. For example, if you're in food service, you run the risk of being sued for food poisoning or some other food-related mishap. Choosing a corporate form would therefore be appropriate in order to protect you against loss of your personal assets. On the other hand, the corporate form can complicate your life in certain ways. State franchise taxes have to be paid; annual meetings must be held; expenses are involved in forming and maintaining the corporation. It represents a less streamlined method of doing business. If you do not foresee the possibility of your business's being sued for liability, or if the business is not going to take on significant debt, it might be best to structure it as a sole proprietorship or partnership. Still, in these days of rampant litigation, it seems to me that all but the simplest of businesses should probably take one of the two corporate forms, "C" or "S."

Activating one of those corporate forms is akin to having a baby: The result of forming a corporation is, in the eyes of the law, another person. That "person" has a fiscal year, the twelve-month period used to measure profitability; calculates and files its own tax return, separate from the tax return that you calculate and file; and has legal name registered with the state.

The birth of this new legal "person" may provide some opportunity for tax savings. The first and most important issue is that in a business environment, losses are deductible. The government has become a partner, not only in your private life but in your business life as well. The government plans to share the profits of your endeavors with you in the form of taxation. But to be somewhat fair, the government is also prepared, to a very limited extent, to share your losses by allowing you to deduct the business expenses that help you to earn revenue. Examples of those expenses include salaries, rent, travel, entertainment, stationery, pens, pencils, legal and accounting services, telephone, electricity, and automobiles. Certain items of equipment, such as automobiles, are deductible over a specified period of time instead of in one lump sum. To whatever extent these items represent a deduction from revenue, they represent a tax savings.

This is no time to get the wrong idea, however. Having deductions that exceed revenue is not usually desirable, since making a profit is the goal of most businesses. In nearly all cases, the old saw that "they need a deduction" is simply untrue. As long as tax rates are less than 100 percent, anybody who generates a tax deduction has lost money, not made money. Revenue that exceeds expenses is generally the sign of a healthy business. Because business expenses are deductible, though, you want to be sure to keep track of all those expenses so you don't pay any more taxes than is absolutely necessary. Part of the process of becoming an entrepreneur includes constructing a system for keeping track of your expenses. Regardless of whether you construct your system with simple tools (e.g., a notebook and pencil) or more elaborate tools (e.g., a computer), adequate record keeping is essential in order to file an accurate tax return—and be able to defend that return in case of an IRS audit.

Modern tax laws says that deductions or business losses can't exceed the investment in the business. If you invest $10,000 in your business and lose $20,000, you can only deduct the $10,000 that you invested. But where did the other $10,000 come from? Did the business take out a loan in order to get the additional $10,000? If it did and subsequently lost the money, why wasn't it deductible? That question leads to precisely the reason why structure is important. If you read Chapter 13, "Funding," you'll remember that I talked about the fact that banks are willing to lend funds to new businesses. They will, as a matter of course, require the business's owners to pledge their assets, both business and personal, as collateral against those loans. Now, in this chapter, I talk about the fact that losses can't exceed the investment in the business. This brings us to a very important conclusion: If you're going to borrow money from the bank to fund your new business, you might want to consider borrowing it as an individual and then loaning it to the corporation. If you do that, instead of having the business obtain the loan directly from the bank, those losses will become fully deductible to you. The loan that you make to the business is considered an investment. The nature of that loan, from the bank's point of view, is the same regardless of whether the money was loaned to the business and collateralized by your assets or the money was loaned to you and collateralized by the business.

The second difference between business taxation and your personal taxation is that with businesses, certain items can cross tax years. That is, businesses can take losses and profits from different periods, whereas your personal income-tax, losses and profits are generally limited to a single year. For example, when you filed your 1987 tax return, you counted all of your income from 1987 and all of your deductions for 1987, arrived at your taxable income, and paid taxes on that amount. Then, you did the same for 1988 and 1989. Those years stood apart from each other, and you couldn't say, "Well, I had lots of deductions in 1987, and I want to apply them to 1988." Your business, however, has some limited ability to do just that. Let's say your business lost money in 1987. That loss can be carried forward to 1988 and be deducted against 1988 revenue. If, in 1988, the business still showed a loss, that loss, together with the preceding year's loss could be carried forward to 1989. If your business generates losses that exceed the income for a given year, those losses can keep being carried forward until, at some point, the business generates a profit. If the venture never generates a profit and you go out of business, the losses are, of course, lost and become unusable. On the other hand, if you didn't deduct those losses on your individual return and your business eventually does generate a profit, the losses that it sustained in the early years will help mitigate any taxes due in later years.

There are other expenses that become deductible to your entrepreneurial business that you could not deduct as a corporate executive. One example is a retirement plan. As a corporate executive, you probably had a retirement plan that was funded mostly or entirely by the corporation. Now that you're an entrepreneur, the corporation is gone, naturally, but your new company can fund the retirement plan for you (and your employees). In most cases, all the funds contributed to that retirement plan become deductible as a business expense. As an entrepreneur, your ability to put money away for retirement is vastly enhanced, since dollars can be saved without any taxes' being paid on them. Furthermore, money in a retirement plan can be invested on a tax-free basis until such time as you take it out. Of course, any funds taken from a retirement plan become taxable upon receipt. Generally speaking, if monies are taken out before you reach age 55, they are subject to both income tax and a 10 percent penalty.

As with all things, it's important to separate the details from what's essential. Saving taxes can become an obsession rather than a strategy. Just as food avoidance is an all-consuming goal to the anorexic, tax avoidance can become an all-consuming goal to the entrepreneur. Here's a good analogy: "Taxes are like the tail of a dog. It's important not to let the tail wag the dog. The dog can live without the tail, but the tail can't live without the dog." Although paying taxes isn't a concern unless your company is profitable, if it *is* profitable, devoting careful attention to tax and structure issues can help you conserve that profit.

Chapter 15

Employee Benefits

Judging from its title, you might think this chapter's subject is of relatively minor importance, compared with the major issues of choosing a business and funding it. However, I have found that employee benefits can be critically important under the following circumstances:

1. If you are over age 45
2. If you are competing with other companies to attract top employees
3. If you have more than a few employees
4. If you are in a position to take advantage of the tax breaks certain plans offer

Even if you are not in one of these four categories, employee benefits are relevant. At some point, you're going to need the benefits that you gave up when you left the corporation, particularly medical and retirement benefits.

Unless you were a human resources executive, your understanding of employee benefits is probably limited. As an entrepreneur, you can't afford such ignorance, as I think you'll see when you read the following pages.

Your Situation

Evaluate where you were, where you are, and where you are going. Past, present, and future will determine your choice of employee benefits. And when I talk about benefits, I'm referring to two basic types of plans: health and retirement. Within each category, there are a variety of choices. Although there are other kinds of benefits, such as stock-option plans, you probably won't have to worry about them for a long time.

During your new business's first year, you may not need or want any type of benefit plan. If, for instance, your former employer covered you under group health insurance, it must offer you a COBRA plan, which is a continuation of your group health insurance, at your cost, for at least eighteen months after your departure date. If your spouse is working, you might be able to get coverage under his or her company's group health plan. Similarly, if you are just getting a new business off the ground, you wouldn't even want to begin worrying about retirement benefits during this start-up phase; you'll need every spare dollar you can find for the business. However, if you fit into one of the four categories listed at the beginning of this chapter, you're a good candidate for some type of plan.

It is important for you to know that the law does not require you to have a health or retirement plan, either for yourself or for your employees, but as I'll discuss later, the government does provide tax incentives for you to do so.

For now, let's concentrate on the different types of plans available.

Health and Medical Insurance

Let's assume you have started a small company with a handful of employees. You decide you must provide them (and yourself) with health insurance because: they expect that coverage as a condition of employment, you need to offer it in order to attract the employees you want to hire, or the cost is affordable and you want to cover yourself and your family.

Before you contact insurance companies about kinds of plans and costs, it might be wise to go through the following glossary of key terms so you will be better-prepared to evaluate the bewildering number of choices and costs that will be offered to you:

▸ *Health Insurance.* This is the broadest term. Typically, health insurance covers any costs that might arise as a result of ill health. Those costs may be related to a hospital bill, loss of income, or both.

▸ *Medical Insurance.* Medical insurance is normally more limited, in that it is specifically aimed at reimbursement of medical expenses. Those expenses might arise from hospitalization, doctors' charges, prescription drugs, therapy, or health-related equipment. Medical insurance is normally provided on one of two bases, group or individual.

▸ *Group Health Insurance.* This is the type of insurance that you probably had with the corporation. Generally, this is a plan provided to all the employees and dependents of a specific organization. With group health insurance, the charges (premiums) are averaged for the entire group. For example, a twenty-two-year-old male employee would probably pay the same premium as a fifty-five-year-old female employee. These uniform premiums are arrived at by using a table that lists a separate premium for each employee according to his or her age and sex. These separate premiums are then totaled and averaged so that all employees are charged at a single rate. The same is true of dependent costs. If your family consisted of only a spouse whereas another employee's family consisted of a spouse and nine children, the premiums would be the same, since the costs for all dependents are averaged. It is important to understand this because, it means that, depending on your situation, the COBRA coverage offered by your employer may or may not be cost-effective. For example, if you are a single, young employee, it may be to your advantage to check into individual insurance as opposed to taking the CO-BRA plan.

▸ *Individual Health Insurance.* As its name implies, individual health insurance is a policy issued by an insurance company on an individual or an individual and his or her family, not as part of a plan covering a specific organization. When you purchase individual health insurance, you are purchasing a policy whose premium generally reflects the insured's age, number and age of dependents, etc., instead of the makeup of a group. Although this may result in an economic

advantage over accepting **COBRA** insurance, issues of insurability and preexisting conditions can enter into that decision.

▸ *Insurability*. This simply means an insurance company's
willingness to take you and/or your family as a risk. The
primary issue affecting insurability is the current physical
health of you and your family. That is, are you or any of your
family suffering from any kind of physical disability or dis-
ease? Factors that are indicative of potential health problems—such as family history, weight, use of alcohol or tobacco,
and even occupation—are also considered. You and all the
members of your family must, in most cases, submit evidence
of insurability to the insurance company. This usually consists
of a relatively detailed questionnaire concerning your and your
family's health history; in addition, a physical exam, blood
tests, and urinalysis may be required.

▸ *Preexisting Condition*. This is a health condition that
exists before the time health insurance is granted. Both individual and group policies usually contain a provision regarding preexisting conditions. Let's say you had a broken arm at
the time you joined a company that had group insurance.
Typically, that group insurance would exclude coverage of any
condition relating to your arm until you had gone for between
six months and one year without treatment. Thereafter, your
arm would probably be covered. In individual health policies,
that six-month to one-year period might be replaced by an
exclusion of your arm from coverage for a stipulated length of
time or even for the life of the policy.

▸ *Hospital Confinement*. In most policies, hospital confinement means just that: a hospital stay lasting one day or longer.
This type of coverage normally pays for charges associated
with the hospital: room and board, operating room, medicine,
special nursing, drugs, and tests. What distinguishes these
charges from other charges that could be incurred during a
hospital stay is that they are for services provided by the
hospital rather than by physicians.

▸ *Surgical Coverage*. Surgical coverage deals with physicians' charges that are related to surgery, generally including
charges by a surgeon, anesthesiologist, and surgical assistants.

Typically, surgical insurance covers pre- and postsurgical charges by those physicians.

▸ *Other Charges.* Other charges usually include those charges not related to hospital confinement or surgery, such as, charges associated with physicians' visits (in or out of the hospital) drugs, health paraphernalia used in the home, X rays, and lab tests.

▸ *Hospital-Indemnity Insurance.* A hospital-indemnity policy generally pays so many dollars per day of hospital confinement as opposed to paying the charges generated by the confinement itself. This is a very important distinction. If you buy a medical-insurance policy, go into the hospital, and run up charges at the rate of $1,000 per day (not very hard to do), that medical-insurance policy presumably pays all or most of the charges that you incur. If, on the other hand, you have a hospital-indemnity policy, the policy only pays up to its maximum amount—e.g., $200 per day. You cannot rely on a hospital-indemnity policy to pay the bills associated with an illness. Such a policy is really designed only to pay extra dollars.

▸ *Disability Insurance.* This type of insurance is typically used to replace income. For example, if you are hospitalized, you not only run up hospital bills at an enormous rate, but you are also losing revenue. That is, you are not working and getting paid. Disability insurance is not designed to pay those medical expenses but to replace the income you are losing because of the sickness. It is normally designed to start paying at a stated point after illness begins and keep paying for a specific period, which may be as long as your lifetime. The cost of disability insurance is related to your age when you purchase the policy, the amount of monthly income you are purchasing, the point at which payments start (the longer the delay, the less expensive the policy), and the length of time for which payments will be made (the longer the time period for which payments will be made, the more expensive the policy).

One of the important issues of disability insurance is the so-called definition of disability. That refers to how the insurance company actually determines that you are disabled. Does "disabled" mean that you can only sell apples on the street

corner, or does the company use a more sophisticated definition? The least sophisticated definition commonly used is that
if you qualify as disabled for purposes of social security, you
are considered to be disabled under the terms of a policy.
Social security regards you as disabled if you have been disabled for six months and will remain disabled, permanently
unable to work at any job that pays you a wage or salary. On
the other hand, under the most sophisticated definition of
disability, you are disabled if you cannot work at your own
occupation. That would mean, for example, that a singer would
be disabled if he or she lost the power of speech or hearing,
and that a surgeon would be disabled if he or she lost the use
of a hand or went blind. Generally, the more sophisticated and
liberal the definition of disability, the more expensive the
policy.

▸ *Major-Medical Insurance.* Major-medical insurance is
meant to cover more expensive illnesses as opposed to small
bills. For example, a major-medical policy would generally not
differentiate between hospital and nonhospital coverage but
instead would lump those all together to provide some level of
coverage. Major-medical insurance usually has deductibles
and coinsurance features. For instance, a major-medical policy
might pay 80 percent of all charges after the policyholder has
paid out $1,000. That means if the bill were $10,000, the
policyholder would pay the first $1,000 and the insurance
company would pay 80 percent of the next $9,000, or $7,200.
The insured would pay 20 percent of that $9,000, or $1,800.
That 20 percent is called coinsurance. Very often, major-medical policies have a stop-loss clause that stipulates that after
the policyholder has paid a total of $5,000 or $10,000, the
insurance company pays 100 percent. Normally, the maximum
coverage with major medical policies is very high, from
$500,000 to $1 million, and in some cases is unlimited.

▸ *Deductible.* In any kind of health insurance, the deductible is simply the amount that the policyholder must pay
before the insurance company begins to pay. It works exactly
the same way as the deductible on automobile collision insurance. If your accident causes $1,000 in damage and you have a

$200 deductible, the insurance company only pays for $800 of the damages. With health insurance, deductibles may be waived in certain situations. For example, many policies that provide family coverage only charge two or three deductibles per family no matter how many family members are covered by the policy.

▸ *Coinsurance.* Coinsurance represents, in percentage terms, how the bill is split between you and the insurance company. A typical coinsurance split is 20 percent for the policyholder and 80 percent for the insurance company. That means the insurance company pays 80 percent of the bill and the policyholder pays 20 percent. Recently, some policies have come on the market, particulary in the group-insurance area, under which the coinsurance paid by the policyholder rises to 30 percent or 40 percent. Of course, the greater the percentage of the bill covered by the policyholder, the lower the premiums. Usually, coinsurance benefits are mitigated by a stop-loss clause so that the policyholder does not have to pay an unlimited amount.

▸ *Stop Loss.* A stop-loss provision in a policy simply means that when a certain level of payment has been reached, the policyholder has no further liability. This is typical with coinsurance provisions, under which the policyholder may be liable for 20 percent of the bill up to X dollars, after which, the insurance company pays 100 percent of the balance. The maximum amount for which the policyholder is liable is usually set at $2,000, $5,000, or $10,000.

▸ *HMO.* The abbreviation *HMO* stands for "health maintenance organization." HMOs are generally associated with a hospital and undertake to provide members with total medical services, from obstetrics to geriatrics. HMOs normally charge a regular monthly premium but have no deductible or coinsurance features. You can visit the doctor or the hospital as often as necessary without paying any deductibles or any part of the bill. Most HMOs have arrangements with local drugstores to provide prescription drugs. When you belong to an HMO, you are usually covered only for HMO member hospitals and physicians. That is, if you go to a physician who is not a member of the HMO or to whom you are not referred by the HMO, that charge is not covered. In addition, even within the HMO, charges are covered only when authorized by a physician. You cannot go to a specialist without your assigned physician's referral.

▸ *PPO.* The abbreviation *PPO* stands for "preferred provider organization." To some extent, a PPO parallels the HMO structure in the private health-insurance community. With a PPO structure, the health-insurance provider, insurance company, or employer imposes a penalty on patients who seek services from physicians or hospitals that do not belong to the PPO group. For example, a health-insurance policy might provide 90 percent coverage for services provided by members of a PPO but only 70 percent coverage for services provided by nonmembers. That means that if you go to a hospital that is part of the preferred provider organization, your insurance picks up 90 percent of your bill, but if you go to a hospital that is not part of that PPO, the insurance only picks up 70 percent of your bill. Unlike an HMO, an insurer usually covers some (normally, most) of a hospital or medical bill from an institution or a physician who is not a PPO member.

Choosing a Health- and Medical-Insurance Plan

For most entrepreneurs, the choices boil down to cost: Which health- and medical-insurance policy will provide you and your employees with adequate coverage at the lowest possible cost?

Here is how to make your estimate. Monthly costs can run $130 per employee and $350 per family for basic health coverage. One way to control this cost is via the deductible: The higher the deductible, the lower the monthly premium. You may also be able to vary the coinsurance—for example, between 20 percent and 40 percent. If you are thinking of providing group insurance for your employees, you should be aware that many cash-starved entrepreneurs opt for catastrophic health coverage. They choose a very high deductible ($500 or more) and a policy that reimburses charges on a coinsurance basis. Another cost-saving approach is to share premium charges between employee and employer. It is not unusual for employers to pick up only a portion of the cost for the employee and none of the cost for his or her dependents. That way, you are offering insurance to your employees but not fully subsidizing its cost. Your choice will depend on your own personal view and the competitive nature of the labor market that you are in.

The cost-saving measures just described should motivate employees to assess their coverage carefully. For instance, employees whose spouses are insured elsewhere will not be encouraged to insure those spouses with your company. In addition, because the real experience (aggregate claims paid) for an employee group affects the cost of coverage, employees have an incentive to avoid unnecessary medical procedures and check medical bills carefully for erroneous charges.

You should also be aware that many group-insurance companies expect you to purchase life insurance along with your health-insurance policy. In many instances, they won't sell you the latter without the former. Although you might be able to buy life-insurance coverage in minimal amounts, it still represents an additional cost.

Retirement Plans

Your former employer probably offered you one or more retirement plans as part of your fringe-benefit package. As an employee, you viewed those plans as vehicles to provide retirement benefits and long-term savings. As an employer, your perspective must change. Not only do these plans help you save for the future, but they can provide you with significant tax breaks and allow you to attract and keep key personnel.

In order to help you decide which plan is best for you, I must again present a glossary of key terms:

▸ *Defined-Benefit Plan.* A defined-benefit plan is designed to provide a percentage of an employee's income, on a monthly basis, to the employee at retirement. The employer makes contributions to the plan based on the income and age of each employee. Generally, the older the employee, the larger the contribution. All contributions to the plan are tax-deductible, and funds in the plan grow tax-free. Most plans use an assumed rate of interest, and earnings in excess of that assumed rate go to reduce plan contributions. By the same token, if earnings are less than the assumed rate of interest, the company makes up the difference. Benefits become taxable only when employees receive the money upon retirement. A defined-benefit plan is what is usually thought of as a pension plan.

▸ *Profit-Sharing Plan.* In a profit-sharing plan, a company makes a contribution, which is then split among the employees according to their income. The monies in a profit-sharing plan go into an account for each employee, and the funds are invested (usually, by the employer). The results of that investment are credited to each employee's account. Profit-sharing plans are based only on income. The greater the salary, the greater the contribution. The company has the option of making no contribution in a given year. The term *profit sharing* is really a misnomer, since a company does not have to be profitable in order to make a contribution, and the contribution may have nothing to do with the company's actual profitability. And the ultimate benefit received by an employee is not predetermined, as it is with a pension plan. Instead, the amount fluctuates based on the contributions made by the company and the investment results.

▸ *401(k).* A 401(k) is a type of profit-sharing plan, with the following differences:

- ▸ Employees can make contributions to the plan (up to 25 percent of their salary, but no more than approximately $8,000).
- ▸ Employees can very often control the investment of the funds and can choose what kind of investments are made with the monies in their own account.
- ▸ An employer can make a contribution to a 401(k) that is contingent on an employee's making a contribution. This is called a matching contribution, and it can provide a very powerful incentive for an employee to contribute to the plan.

Choosing a Retirement Plan

Here are some rules of thumb that can help you select a plan that is right for you, your employees, and your business. Before getting involved in choosing a retirement plan, however, remember that cash is king. Your company should be generating enough revenue to sustain itself and you and your family before you consider any type of retirement plan, unless specific conditions require you to do so. Tax benefits, personal retirement savings, and incentives for employees are not as important as a profitable, self-sustaining business.

If you are over 45 and decide you need a plan, a defined-benefit plan is generally right for you; it offers more security and the opportunity to put more money away than any other kind of plan. If you are under age 45 and have relatively few employees, a profit-sharing plan may be right for you; it offers a great deal of flexibility and relative simplicity.

If you have a large number of employees, a profit-sharing plan with a 401(k) is a good choice. It provides for maximum employee participation and flexibility, in that the employees can control their own accounts, while not making any additional demands on you as an employer. Because of the antidiscrimination rules associated with a 401(k), it is not suitable for very small companies with only a few employees.

Many of you will postpone deciding about a retirement plan until you have run your business for a year and determined how successful the venture has been. Let's assume it did reasonably well. Take 25 percent of your salary and then compare that figure to the leftover cash—the money that remains after you have paid your expenses. If your leftover amount is greater than the 25 percent figure, put it in a defined-benefit plan. If it is less than 25 percent, you could put it either in a defined-benefit plan or in a profit-sharing plan with a 401(k).

The amount you put in is, in part, related to your tax bracket. Remember, contributions to any kind of retirement plan are tax-deductible. Supposing you are in the 31 percent tax bracket with a 2 percent state tax, making your total tax bracket 33 percent. If you put $10,000 in a retirement plan, you are really contributing only $6,600. If you had taken the $10,000 in salary and paid $3,300 in taxes, you would have had $6,600 left. When you examine the result of the retirement plan, how much of that $10,000 contribution is going to you? If $6,600 or more of the total contribution is going to you, the retirement plan, *by itself*, is profitable. That is, you have taken $3,300 of potential tax money and put it into your pocket and those of your employees instead of Uncle Sam's coffers. That does not count the investment yield on those funds or the fact that while the money is in the plan, that investment yield is untaxed. A general rule is to put as much money into a retirement plan as you possibly can. Monies that go into a plan are contributed tax-free and grow tax-free, and while they are in the plan, are safe from creditors. As long as the dollars you contribute to a plan are equal to or more than the posttax dollars you would have received had you taken the contribution as salary or a bonus, that contribution generates a profit in dollars and employee morale.

This is not to say that contributions to a retirement plan should replace regular savings or a cash cushion. Remember that it is considerably harder to get money out of a retirement plan before retirement than it is to make a withdrawal from a regular savings account. You should therefore maintain a certain amount of savings and investments outside of your retirement plan in order to provide cash for unexpected situations.

By and large, though, retirement plans are the last, and still the best, tax shelter. They allow you to effectively transfer money from one pocket to another while taking a tax deduction in the process. As a business owner rather than an employee, you are in an excellent position to take advantage of that shelter.

Chapter 16

Keeping Your Eyes and Options Open

One last bit of advice I'd like to offer is to remember that things change. If it weren't for the changes that have taken place in the last two decades, this book would be unnecessary. Most of you would never have thought of leaving your secure corporate offices for the unfamiliar world of entrepreneurship. But things have changed, and you've seen how social, economic, and technological developments can make once-secure jobs precarious or obsolete.

Whether you've already made the transition from executive to entrepreneur or are simply considering making it, keep your eyes open for further changes. They are inevitable, and they will impact your decisions. A recession, a sudden end to the downsizing trend, new laws unfavorable to small businesses—any of these developments may affect your entrepreneurial aspirations. Or they may not. Everyone will be affected differently. Ultimately, your decision to strike out on your own is an intensely personal one. Not only do you have to be aware of the changes going on around you, but you have to determine how they affect your specific situation.

How strong is your desire to become an entrepreneur? Do you really hate working for someone else, or are your negative feelings temporary, the result of being abruptly terminated or some other event? The way you answer these questions can also change, based on your growth as an individual as well as external events. After a few years as an entrepreneur, you may find that you prefer working for someone else. Given an upturn in the economy, scores of job opportunities might suddenly blossom within corporations. Or you might move from one entrepreneurial business to another. It's possible that your first business could fail. If you still have the drive to be an entrepreneur, a second or even a third business might be your ticket to entrepreneurial success.

Think of two types of dogs. One is a porch-sitting hound who isn't disturbed by anything, who can't be roused from his favorite spot by man or beast. The other is a terrier, its ears alway perked up, reacting to the slightest sound or movement. Be the terrier. Keep alert for whatever changes are taking place around you. The more you perceive, the better your ability to determine whether an executive or entrepreneurial work style meets your needs.

Years ago, such a determination wasn't called for. Then, business school followed by tenure at a major corporation were common goals. The relative few who became entrepreneurs rarely did so by making a switch from corporate employee—*entrepreneurs* and *MBAs* seemed contradictory terms. Although it's easier now to make the switch, it's difficult to decide whether you should, when you should, and what you should switch to. Even after you've made the decision to become an entrepreneur and have set yourself up in business, numerous decisions still await you. Many of those decisions will be affected by your years as a corporate employee—you can't simply dismiss everything you've learned during that period.

Nor should you want to. Most executive-entrepreneurs find their corporate background to be a double-edged sword: It can both help and hinder their efforts as independent businesspeople. One of my objectives in writing this book has been to help you wield that sword effectively but selectively. Throughout these chapters, I've provided anecdotes and examples of people who have gone before you. I've spotlighted the mistakes they made as well as the opportunities they seized. More important, I've focused on how their corporate background affected their entrepreneurship, both positively and negatively.

How will your background affect you? As the financial wizards say, the upside potential outweighs the downside risk. If the golden age of entrepreneurs dawns as expected, you'll be in an excellent position to capitalize on your years as a corporate executive. That experience, combined with a sincere desire to run your own show, gives you advantages that past entrepreneurs lacked.

Much of this book has been designed to help you answer the questions, "Should I remain an executive or become an entrepreneur?" To enable you to find an answer, I've provided numerous checklists and scenarios that require you to project yourself into an entrepreneurial setting. Such projection is fine, but it's no substitute for the real thing. Most of you won't know for sure whether you're cut out to be an independent businessperson until you try it. Once you're on your own, you'll quickly get a sense of whether it's right for you. That doesn't guarantee a successful business, though. You may find that you love being an entrepreneur but the business you've chosen isn't viable.

What does the future hold for the executive-entrepreneur? Will the decade of the nineties provide a favorable climate for this hybrid businessperson? More than one aspiring entrepreneur has asked me this question, and my answer invariably is: It doesn't matter. At least, it doesn't matter from an individual's perspective. If you want to leave your company and set up your own business, then do it! If you have an idea for a business and the money to make it happen, then make it happen! Don't become trapped by an article that predicts bad times ahead for entrepreneurs or studies that show an alarming failure rate among new businesses. Those articles and studies have appeared every year—in good times as well as bad.

You can't control the future, so don't try. All you can control is your decision about what type of work environment suits you best. If you have decided to stay in the executive ranks, I hope this book has helped you focus on your talents and needs. If you have decided to start your own business, I wish you good fortune as you join the growing ranks of a new class of entrepreneur.

Index

[Italic page numbers refer to figures.]